THE STALIN DICTATORSHIP

Khrushchev's 'Secret Speech'
and Other Documents

THE STALIN DICTATORSHIP

Khrushchev's 'Secret Speech'
and Other Documents

Edited, with Introduction and Annotations, by
T. H. RIGBY

SYDNEY UNIVERSITY PRESS

SYDNEY UNIVERSITY PRESS
Press Building, University of Sydney

U.S.A. Pennsylvania State University Press
NEW ZEALAND Price Milburn and Company Limited
ELSEWHERE Methuen and Company Limited, London
and their agents

Introduction and annotations copyright 1968 by T. H. Rigby
First published 1968

National Library of Australia registry number AUS 67-661
Library of Congress Catalog Card Number 68-21928

This book is supported by money from
THE ELEANOR SOPHIA WOOD BEQUEST

Printed by The Specialty Press Limited,
611 Blackburn Road, North Clayton, Victoria,
and registered in Australia for transmission by post as a book

CONTENTS

Preface   7

Introduction   11

N. S. Khrushchev: 'On the Cult of Personality
    and its Consequences'   23

Resolution of the 20th Congress of the CPSU   91

Khrushchev Returns to the Attack   93

A 17th Congress Delegate on the Proposal to Replace
    Stalin and the Murder of Kirov   109

A Case History in Soviet Decision-Making under Stalin   113

Further Reading   121

Index   123

PREFACE

Personal dictatorship exercised through a series of bureaucratic apparatuses permeating wide aspects of social life has been one of the commonest types of political system in the twentieth century. Moreover, while there appears to be a tendency in more industrialized societies for such personal dictatorships to be transformed into systems with a more oligarchical, diffuse or even pluralistic exercise of power, new bureaucratic dictatorships are constantly being generated as 'development' disrupts the traditional polities of less industrialized societies.

Communist states have not always functioned as bureaucratic dictatorships, but they have supplied the largest single group of such dictatorships. The 'type case' of the communist dictatorship is, of course, the U.S.S.R. under Stalin. Study of how power was exercised in Stalinist Russia should therefore be instructive for a whole class of modern political systems as numerous and important, perhaps, as the 'liberal', 'pluralistic' or 'capitalist' democracies.

In Stalin's lifetime such study was greatly hampered by the lack of primary source material, particularly relating to the upper reaches of power. Since his death, a good deal of information has emerged, most notably in Khrushchev's 'secret speech' to the Twentieth Congress of the Soviet Communist Party, but in other places as well. It is in order to make the relevant documents available to students of politics in convenient form that the present book has been compiled. In the Introduction and annotations, the content and timing of Khrushchev's revelations are also analysed for their relevance to Soviet politics in the post-Stalin era.

The text of the available version of the 'secret speech' is given here in full, in view of its many-sided importance which is discussed in the Introduction. In the selection and excerpting of other documents, I have sought to expand on the material contained in the 'secret speech' on two main topics: the connection

7

of the 'Kirov Affair' with the challenge to Stalin's power and the consolidation of his dictatorship in the middle 1930s, and the role and position of members of the dictator's inner circle and his senior officials in the Stalinist system.

In approaching this material, the student is recommended first to establish what generalizations Khrushchev makes about the character of the Soviet political system under Stalin's dictatorship, and then to consider how far these generalizations are established or need to be modified or supplemented, by the information contained in the documents.

To Professor Henry Mayer, of the University of Sydney, I owe the idea of this book. I am particularly grateful to Paul Rosta, of the London School of Economics and Political Science, who thoroughly checked the text and made numerous valuable suggestions. It wish also to thank Mrs Natalie Staples, especially for preparing the index, and Mrs K. Tinnion and Mrs B. Coles for coping cheerfully and efficiently with a messy manuscript while the perpetrator was on the wing. The editor naturally accepts full responsibility for any remaining errors, infelicities or lapses of judgement.

T.H.R.

THE STALIN DICTATORSHIP

Introduction

Khrushchev's report 'On the Cult of Personality and its Consequences', delivered to the 20th Congress of the Communist Party of the Soviet Union (CPSU) on 25 February 1956, is a document of major importance for the study of Soviet political history and the operation of the Soviet political system. Its importance is compounded of a number of elements.

Most obviously, the report contains several previously unknown facts, such as the number of Central Committee members and Seventeenth Congress delegates who perished in the 1937-8 terror (p. 37), the aborted Central Committee meeting in October 1941 (p. 36), Stalin's method of governing through sub-committees of the Politburo (pp. 80-1) and his threats against older party leaders on the eve of his death (p. 81). Of course, we have only Khrushchev's word, the word of an interested participant, on these matters. However, what he says is intrinsically plausible and consistent with other known facts. Moreover, while his personal interest clearly conditioned his selection and emphasis of facts to report, the political circumstances of the occasion would have made it extremely difficult actually to falsify the facts.

Secondly, Khrushchev offers here 'official' confirmation, complete or partial, of a number of matters on which our knowledge previously rested only on the testimony of Stalin's rivals and critics or on deductions made from circumstantial evidence. Such matters include Lenin's antagonism to Stalin on the eve of his death (p. 26), Stalin's complicity in the murder of Kirov (p. 39), his jealousy of Marshal Zhukov after World War II (p. 60), the 'Leningrad affair' (p. 62), and the connection between the reorganization of the central party machinery in 1952 and his intended purge of the party leadership (p. 82). On some of these matters, notably the events surrounding the murder of Kirov, additional information has subsequently appeared in Soviet sources. Khrushchev returned to the Kirov murder in his report to the 22nd Congress in 1961, and further revelations were made in an article by L. Shaumian, published in *Pravda* in 1964. Translations of the relevant sections of these documents are included in this book.

Extremely little has been written by actual participants about the higher reaches of Soviet political life. Unlike some British prime ministers, no Soviet statesman has yet devoted an honoured retirement to composing his memoirs. The only substantial participant reports are provided by Stalin's archrival Leon Trotsky, but these, important as they are, cover only the first decade of the Soviet régime and even for this period leave vast and tantalizing gaps. The Menshevik writer Boris Nicolaevsky, in his *Letter of an Old Bolshevik,* has conveyed the gist of Nikolai Bukharin's observations of developments in the early 1930s, but by this time Bukharin was already excluded from the inner circles of the leadership. This dearth of participant accounts indicates a third significance of Khrushchev's report, which includes a number of personal reminiscences about his experiences as a member of Stalin's Politburo. Of course Khrushchev is concerned in these passages to present matters in the best possible light for himself. However, self-justification is a generally recognized failing of all memoirists. It does not nullify their value as sources, though it demands some care and skill in using them. Other than these reminiscences of Khrushchev's, interesting light is thrown on decision-making processes and the political atmosphere under Stalin by some brief memoirs published by one of his ministers, B. L. Vannikov, which we have excerpted in this book.[1]

Khrushchev's 'Cult of Personality' report, however, is important not only for the light it throws on the Stalin era. It constituted a potent political act of the utmost significance for the whole future development of the U.S.S.R., and indeed of the communist movement throughout the world. To appreciate this we must recall some background facts.

Following Stalin's death in March 1953 no Soviet leader succeeded in laying hold of his enormous personal powers, though Malenkov attempted to, and so, too, probably, did Beria. Instead, power was shared within an oligarchy of former Politburo members calling themselves 'the Presidium of the Central Committee'. In their efforts to strengthen their 'collective leadership' the oligarchs were soon forced to modify important ideological and organizational aspects of Stalin's system of personal rule, most notably by curbing the leadership cult and the arbitrary powers of the political police. Radical steps were taken to ease the international situation, and relations were re-established with Tito, execrated under Stalin as a traitor to communism. Meanwhile amongst the population at large, the numbness and disorientation produced by the death of 'the beloved father and teacher' began to give way to a mood of revulsion against the fear, obscurantism and deprivations of the Stalin era. Every step taken by the oligarchy to normalize daily life tended to reinforce rather than to moderate this mood, and it was given a powerful boost by the first tentative efforts of writers and scholars to deal honestly with the Stalin era, and by the stream of relatives and friends returning from Stalin's labour camps after years of torment for non-existent political crimes.

Thus it began to dawn on ordinary Russians that their leaders did not believe what they had said, and had forced others to say, about Stalin and his régime when he was alive, that they now thought his methods of rule were (at least in some respects) wrong, and implicitly admitted that terrible things had been done in his name. Still not a single honest word had yet been spoken by the leaders on these matters, and Stalin remained enthroned in the official pantheon, along with Marx, Engels and Lenin.

Thus the 20th Congress opened in February 1956 in a public atmosphere of considerable confusion and expectation. The political images and formulas in which a whole generation had been reared and matured were now seriously called in question: would new ones be provided? Would the honest word be spoken? As the dreary stereotyped reports and 'debate' on the work of the Central Committee and the new five-year plan dragged on through their second week it seemed that it would not. But then, on the day the congress was due to close, came Khrushchev's report 'On the Cult of Personality and its Consequences'. What had happened?

There is little point in our adding to the existing speculation about the tussles within the leadership over the issue of condemning Stalin (*see* Further Reading, p. 122). It is fairly certain that the decision to give a major report on the issues at the congress was taken only at the last moment. The text gives ample evidence of hasty editing, although it seems apparent that the leadership had been gathering material on the subject for some time. The fact that the conventions of discussion from the floor and of an extended point-by-point resolution were violated (p. 91) is also indicative of last-minute preparation and tends to confirm that the question was not originally included in the congress agenda. Nor would it be surprising if the oligarchy had failed to agree on the content of a critique of Stalin, or even on whether or not to make such a critique. On the latter issue, Molotov and Kaganovich were almost certainly opposed and Mikoyan in favour (he was the only leader to criticize Stalin directly in the open sessions of the congress); others may have been uncertain. As to *what* was to be said, obviously this would affect the reputations (and thereby the future fortunes) of different leaders in different ways and degrees, in view of the varying nature of their careers under Stalin, and the task of securing agreement was therefore formidable indeed. The balance of forces within the oligarchy, moreover, was clearly a delicate one, as is indicated by the fact that the full (voting) membership of the Presidium remained unchanged after the 20th Congress.

It is by no means certain that Khrushchev was initially one of the leaders pressing for an 'honest word'. Indeed it has been suggested that he was in effect forced into his critique by Mikoyan and possibly other ardent de-Stalinizers.[2] Be this as it may, Khrushchev's position on this issue was undoubtedly a most sensitive one. He was now the most powerful man in the oligarchy. In 1954 he had defeated Malenkov in a tussle for *primus inter pares,* and in 1955 had won important organizational and policy disputes with his principal rivals. His protégés had been moved into many key positions, and now numbered something like a third of those entitled to 'full' Central Committee membership — the 'parliament' of the Soviet Communist Party. Despite all this, the other oligarchs were still far from being reduced to 'yes-men', and could still destroy him politically if they chose to combine against him. Meanwhile there were the glaring parallels between the growth of Khrushchev's power and that of Stalin in the 1920s. Like Stalin, Khrushchev had accumulated power mainly by vigorous exploitation of the patronage opportunities afforded by control of the Central Committee secretariat, while manoeuvring to isolate and discredit his principal rivals in the leadership and at the same time building up the 'full' Central Committee to potentially outflank his fellow-oligarchs. Any attack on Stalin's career and methods, therefore, contained special risks for Khrushchev, for he alone among the 'collective leadership' could be plausibly accused of currently attempting to 'do a Stalin'.

While we can only guess at the line taken by Khrushchev within the leadership on this issue, it was obvious that once he decided that a major attack on Stalin could not be avoided, he would have to give a lead to it. As First Secretary, this was his right, and to cede this right to others would mean not only missing the chance to give it a twist of his own, but also inviting suspicions of his nurturing Stalinist proclivities himself, suspicions to which he was uniquely vulnerable for the reasons just mentioned. At the same time, any attack on Stalin emphatic enough to preclude subsequent accusations of 'praising him with faint damns' held the danger of unleashing forces which would be hard to control and for which the First Secretary would be held responsible. Khrushchev had the courage to grasp this nettle. In so doing he committed himself to riding the wave of popular revulsion against Stalinism, to pursuing a pattern of rule purged of the personal arbitrariness, oppression and obscurantism of the past, at a time when powerful forces within the régime entertained the profoundest misgivings against such a course. It was the tactical skill, energy and daring with which he managed this role that won him the dominant position he enjoyed in Soviet political life for the next eight years.

Khrushchev gave to his 'Cult of Personality' report a directness and earthiness, a personal flavour and emotional force, of which no other Soviet leader had shown himself capable, and this undoubtedly reinforced the impact of the speech. At the same time the report is lacking in even a perfunctory attempt at Marxist analysis, and while this was probably due largely to the difficulty of getting the oligarchy to agree on explanatory or theoretical formulations, and on the haste with which the report was evidently edited, it is difficult not to see in this, as well, the untheoretical, commonsensical Khrushchev style.

The two banal and evasive formulas in terms of which both Khrushchev's exposition and the congress resolution were couched — the 'cult of personality' and 'collective leadership' — were part of the doctrinal stock-in-trade of the régime well before the 20th Congress. So far, however, there was only the *implication* that there had been too much of the former and not enough of the latter in the past and these defects had never been explicitly blamed on Stalin. It was left to Khrushchev to supply the crucial factual link between these two formulas: Stalin's conversion of the 'collective leadership' into a system of arbitrary personal rule. Here at last, was an 'honest word': one, however, which must have had a bitter taste for many a Soviet citizen; for there was scarcely a hint of regret at the untold sufferings Stalin's policies had inflicted on tens of millions of ordinary people — it was only when he turned against his loyal supporters that he invited serious condemnation. Moreover, the report lacked not only a Marxist analysis, but *any* historical explanation of how and why Stalin managed to accumulate such 'immense and limitless power', apart from his personal defects of character: his brutality, vindictiveness and megalomania. As contemporary observers were quick to point out, this was merely to turn the 'personality cult' on its head.

The oligarchy, of course, had every reason to limit their critique of Stalinism to a personal attack on Stalin, for only thus could they avoid impugning the legitimacy of the political and social system and their own role in it. Indeed, the congress resolution and Khrushchev's report took pains to stress the legitimacy of the basic elements in the system. They reaffirmed the 'norms of party life and the principles of collective leadership worked out by the Great Lenin', i.e. the basic structure of Soviet political institutions and relationships as established since the early 1920s, which included the single-party system and the dictatorship of the Politburo over the party, exercised through the centralized party apparatus — still all-important elements in their own pattern of rule. Meanwhile Khrushchev explicitly indicated the propriety of Stalin's struggles against the various 'oppositions' of the 1920s and his subsequent measures of farm-collectivization and forced industrialization which laid the foundations of the present economic structure of the U.S.S.R.

While, however, this vindication of the existing order must have enjoyed the unanimous support of the oligarchy, it had special advantages for Khrushchev which he ably exploited. It enabled him to ignore the dimension of personal power-struggle — with its unfortunate contemporary parallels — when referring to Stalin's campaigns against the 'oppositions'. He stated explicitly that 'in the first period after Lenin's death [i.e. the period when Stalin was using the same organizational and tactical techniques to accumulate power as Khrushchev himself was now using] Stalin still paid attention to his advice', i.e. about not abusing the power of Central Committee secretaryship. In Khrushchev's account, it was only *after* these techniques had won for Stalin overwhelming dominance within the leadership that he began to behave reprehensibly, and this was because of a fatal flaw in his character which had earlier been highlighted by his scandalous treatment of Lenin's wife. The problem, then, was not to limit the enormous power conferred by the party secretaryship, but to entrust this power to a man able, in Lenin's words, 'to use this power with the required care'. And by implication he, as the indicter of Stalin's abuses and the sponsor of collective leadership in the Central Committee, was such a man. Khrushchev's stress on the 'full' Central Committee as a bulwark against 'the cult of the individual' has special significance not devoid of a certain irony. From the early 1920s the real locus of 'collective leadership' lay not in the Central Committee, but in its Politburo, just as it lay after 1953 in the Presidium. As already noted, Stalin deliberately fostered the Central Committee, which he could dominate through his patronage, in order to use it against his Politburo rivals, and Khrushchev was engaged in much the same operation. In June 1957, just sixteen months after the 20th Congress, when a majority of the 'collective leadership' attempted to curb Khrushchev, he was able to employ the 'full' Central Committee to defeat this challenge and establish his personal dominance over the leadership, now purged of his main critics.

It was by this careful circumscription and angling of his attack that Khrushchev principally sought to turn the indictment of Stalin to his advantage. More obviously related to this end were the several references to existing leaders. His rivals Kaganovich and Malenkov, like the 'traitor' Beria, are shown as being particularly close to Stalin (pp. 39, 58, 70). He himself is pictured attempting to stand up to the dictator (p. 60), as is his fellow-de-Stalinizer Mikoyan (p. 59). He takes great pains to dissociate himself from the purges in the Ukraine, where he was party secretary at the time (pp. 48, 83). He and his ally Bulganin (now Prime Minister, later to join the unsuccessful 1957 coalition against Khrushchev) are shown privately discussing the difficulties of their situations as members of Stalin's entourage (p. 80), thus hinting at the existence of a 'healthy core' in the leadership which kept the Leninist traditions of the party alive through the Stalin era. Subsequently, at the 22nd CPSU Congress, Khrush-

17

B

chev attempted more openly to tar his rivals with the Stalin brush (pp. 96-100).

The repercussions of the 20th Congress attack on Stalin are too familiar to require extensive treatment here. Although the Soviet leaders sought to limit these repercussions by avoiding publication of Khrushchev's report in the press and in the official transcript of the congress (and thereby getting it labelled Khrushchev's 'secret speech') its main lines quickly became known to wide circles of the Soviet public, in the 'people's democracies' of Eastern Europe, and — after its release to the Western press by the U.S. State Department — to communists throughout the world. The ferment it caused in the Soviet Union itself, confined mainly to students and intellectuals, never assumed dangerous proportions, and was well under control by the middle of 1957. In Eastern Europe, where communism had far weaker roots and the revolt against Stalinism quickly merged into an assertion of national identity against Soviet domination, the ferment developed more quickly and spread more widely, producing by October 1956 a bloodless revolt in Poland and a bloody one in Hungary. In the non-communist world, the 'secret speech' formed a major episode in a continuing — and on the whole favourable — transformation of the Soviet Union's public image; it was a serious blow to the local communist parties, however, and there were vast membership losses, which received a further impetus from the events in Poland and Hungary.

The impact of the 20th Congress was felt on three main levels.

Firstly, there was the profound disorientation caused by discrediting the man who had formed the emotional-symbolic core of the communist movement for nearly 30 years, and on whose worship a whole generation had been reared; what the Soviet leaders were doing might be compared with telling a Christian audience that while the doctrine and institutions of the church were still sacred, Christ himself was a despicable imposter.

Secondly, despite the care taken to vindicate the system while attacking Stalin, the call to 'overcome . . . the cult of personality, to liquidate its consequences in all fields of party, state and ideological work' immediately called in question the whole pattern of communist institutions, behaviour patterns and doctrines, for which aspect of these was not marked with the effects of Stalin's abuse of power?

The third level of impact, though less obvious in the immediate aftermath of the congress, was in the long run the most potent. Khrushchev's failure to attempt any serious explanation of the phenomena of Stalinism, the transparently illogical and hypocritical labelling of these phenomena as '*consequences* of the cult of personality' when the cult itself, even in Khrushchev's account, was at least largely due to Stalin's arbitrary power, were obvious to all thoughtful communists. To leave the problem at this point, in the words of the Italian communist leader Palmiro Togliatti, was to 'remain within the realm of the "personality cult" . . . outside the criterion of judgment intrinsic in Marxism'. And Togliatti went on: 'The true problems are evaded, which are why and how Soviet society could reach and did reach certain forms alien to the democratic way and to the legality which it had set for itself, even to the point of degeneration'.[3] Togliatti called on 'our Soviet comrades' to undertake a Marxist analysis of Stalinism. They never did so, either at that time or since, and in abdicating this responsibility they destroyed the infallible authority not just of Stalin, as was intended, but of the CPSU. At the same time, communists throughout the world, in the absence of an agreed and authoritative evaluation of Stalinism, were free — and sometimes obliged — to come to terms with it in the light of local party needs and experience, and to make their own evaluation of what was of universal validity, what was justifiable by specifically local conditions, and what was 'degenerate' in Soviet institutions and policies. In this way what was *not* said at the 20th Congress, no less than what *was* said, delivered an irreparable blow to the 'monolithic', Moscowcentric unity of the world communist movement, and promoted that diversity, which — most dramatically in the hostility between the U.S.S.R. and China, but in innumerable other ways as well — has so transformed international relations in the last decade. And here we should note that once this process of diversification got under way, it became even more difficult to reach an agreed Marxist analysis; the chances of such an agreed analysis have long been negligible.

The long-term impact of the 20th Congress condemnation of Stalin on the Soviet Union itself has been wholly favourable. It resulted in no institutional changes, though it confirmed those that had already occurred, especially the abolition of personal dictatorship and the curbing of police terror. While Khrushchev capitalized on it to consolidate his own dominance over the leadership, it then obstructed his further advance to a Stalin-type dictatorship* and, ironically, in due course facilitated his removal and the restoration of 'collective leadership'. At a deeper level, it shook the population, and particularly its *élite* segments, from that torpor and passivity which the long years of obscurantism and tyranny had induced, and promoted a degree of rationalization of institutions, ideology and policies that was both made possible, and urgently required, by the country's economic and educational progress. Thus 'the decisions of the 20th CPSU Congress' became symbolic of the more civilized and humane quality of life which the Soviet Union has acquired in the last decade in contradiction to the fear, mendacity and squalor that preceded it. So potent was this symbol, so profound the feelings it evoked, that the Soviet leadership in removing Khrushchev in 1964 felt constrained to reassure the population of their continued adherence to the decisions of the 20th CPSU Congress, thereby provoking Peking's comment that they simply stood for 'Khrushchevism without Khrushchev'.

The original Russian text of Khrushchev's 'personality cult' report has never been published. The only available version, which we have reproduced here, was an English translation released by the United States Department of State on 4 June 1956, with the following introduction.

> The Department of State has recently obtained from a confidential source a copy of a document which purports to be a version of the speech of Party First Secretary N. S. Khrushchev at a session of the XXth Party Congress of the Communist Party of the Soviet Union on February 25, 1956. This session was limited in attendance to the delegates from the U.S.S.R.
>
> The document is being released in response to many inquiries. This version is understood to have been prepared for the guidance of the party leadership of a Communist Party outside of the U.S.S.R. The Department of State does not vouch for the authenticity of the document and in releasing it intends that the document speak for itself.

* We beg, here, the question whether Khrushchev *wanted* to be a dictator, and the role of more 'objective' factors in obstructing this, if he did want it.

20

In fact, the authenticity of this version is beyond serious doubt. It corresponds with contemporary accounts of the speech obtained from Eastern European sources by Reuters' News Service and the Yugoslav communist party newspaper *Borba,* and, more importantly, its authenticity has subsequently been implicitly admitted in many conversations between Soviet representatives and foreigners. It is thought possible, however, that the present version, intended as it was for a non-Soviet audience, may omit some details of the speech as originally delivered.

The State Department translation, perhaps due to a certain haste as well as to a concern to keep as literally close to the original as possible, frequently lapses into awkward and some-times ungrammatical or ambiguous English. Lacking access to the original, an editor can correct this to only a minor degree. Fortunately, the manifest literalness of the translation often indicates beyond doubt what the Russian original must be, and in such cases correction is possible. This particularly applies to the use of definite and indefinite articles (Russian has neither) and the translator's choice of tenses (English has, for instance, seven tenses to render the two past aspectual forms of Russian), as well as to certain recurrent synonyms. Earlier editions of the report have either reproduced the State Department translation unaltered (e.g. the Columbia University Russian Institute's *The Anti-Stalin Campaign and International Communism*) with a few spasmodic amendments (e.g. the *Manchester Guardian*'s *The Dethronement of Stalin*) or with more systematic corrections of the kind indicated above (Bertram D. Wolfe's *Khrushchev and Stalin's Ghost*). It is the last of these courses that we have adopted here, with the working rule, however, that less than 100 per cent certainty about the original precludes amendment; this has meant leaving not a few infelicities. We have also employed somewhat different conventions of abbreviation and nomencla-ture in references to Soviet institutions. Where Khrushchev quotes documents that were subsequently published in the fifth edition of Lenin's *Polnoe Sobranie Sochinenii* — referred to here-after as *Sochineniia* (Collected Works) — translations have been checked against the Russian originals.

One final comment on the translation of the phrase *kul't lich-nosti. Lichnost'* may mean personality, person, individual, accord-ing to context. The State Department translation 'cult of the individual' is the best rendering of the phrase, and we have retained it in our text; however, 'cult of personality', or 'personality cult' quickly became conventional in English, hence its use in our Introduction. The less coy version *kul't lichnosti Stalina* current in the 1960s demands 'personality' or, better still, 'person'.

NOTES

1. V. S. Emelyanov, another senior industrial administrator in the later Stalin era, provides further glimpses at top decision-making processes at this period in his memoirs 'O vremeni, o tovarish-chakh, o sebe; zapiski inzhenera' ('On Time, Comrades and Myself: Notes of an Engineer') *Novyi Mir*, Moscow, Nos 1 and 2, 1967.

2. *See* George Paloczi-Horvath, *Khrushchev: The Road to Power*, pp. 203-4. Khrushchev was later to claim that Molotov, Kaganovich, Malenkov, Voroshilov 'and others' opposed raising the 'personality cult' issue at the congress, and only capitulated when 'we' threatened to appeal over their heads to the congress delegates. (*See* p. 96.)

3. From an interview published in the Italian periodical *Nuovi Argomenti*, No. 20, 16 June 1956, reproduced in *The Anti-Stalin Campaign and International Communism: A Selection of Documents*, pp. 120-1.

N. S. Khrushchev:
'On the Cult of Personality and its Consequences'
Report delivered to the 20th Congress of the CPSU
on 25 February 1956

COMRADES! In the report of the Central Committee of the party at the 20th Congress, in a number of speeches by delegates to the Congress, as well as before this during plenary sessions of the CPSU Central Committee, quite a lot has been said about the cult of the individual and about its harmful consequences.

After Stalin's death the Central Committee of the party began to implement a policy of explaining concisely and consistently that it is impermissible and foreign to the spirit of Marxism-Leninism to elevate one person, to transform him into a superman possessing supernatural characteristics akin to those of a god. Such a man supposedly knows everything, sees everything, thinks for everyone, can do anything, and is infallible in his behaviour.

This kind of belief about a man, namely about Stalin, was cultivated among us for many years.

The objective of the present report is not a thorough evaluation of Stalin's life and activity. Concerning Stalin's merits, a quite sufficient number of books, pamphlets and studies has already been written in his lifetime. The role of Stalin in the preparation and carrying out of the Socialist Revolution, in the Civil War, and in the fight for the construction of Socialism in our country is universally known. Everyone knows this well. At the present we are concerned with a question which has immense importance for the party now and for the future — [we are concerned] with how the cult of the person of Stalin gradually grew, the cult which became at a certain specific stage the source of a whole series of exceedingly serious and grave perversions of party principles, of party democracy, of revolutionary legality.

Because of the fact that not all as yet fully realize the practical consequences resulting from the cult of the individual, the great harm caused by the violation of the principle of collective direction of the party and because of the accumulation of immense and limitless power in the hands of one person — the Central Committee of the party considers it absolutely necessary to make the material pertaining to this matter available to the 20th Congress of the Communist Party of the Soviet Union.

Allow me first of all to remind you how severely the classics of Marxism-Leninism denounced every manifestation of the cult of the individual. In a letter to the German political worker, Wilhelm Bloss, Marx stated:

> Out of my antipathy to any cult of the individual, I never made public during the existence of the International the numerous addresses from various countries which recognized my merits and which annoyed me. I did not even reply to them, except sometimes to rebuke their authors. Engels and I first joined the secret society of Communists on the condition that everything making for superstitious worship of authority would be deleted from its statute. Lassalle subsequently did quite the opposite.

Some time later Engels wrote:

> Both Marx and I have always been against any public manifestation with regard to individuals, with the exception of cases when it had an important purpose; and we most strongly opposed such manifestations which during our lifetime concerned us personally.

The great modesty of the genius of the revolution, Vladimir Ilyich Lenin, is known. Lenin always stressed the role of the people as the creator of history, the directing and organizational role of the party as a living and creative organism, and also the role of the Central Committee.

Marxism does not negate the role of the leaders of the workers' class in directing the revolutionary liberation movement.

While ascribing great importance to the role of the leaders and organizers of the masses, Lenin at the same time mercilessly stigmatized every manifestation of the cult of the individual, inexorably combated views which are foreign to Marxism, about the 'hero' and the 'crowd', and countered all efforts to oppose the 'hero' to the masses and to the people.

24

Lenin taught that the party's strength depends on its indissoluble unity with the masses, on the fact that behind the party follow the people — workers, peasants and intelligentsia. 'Only he will win and retain the power', said Lenin, 'who believes in the people, who submerges himself in the fountain of the living creativeness of the people'.

Lenin spoke with pride about the Bolshevik Communist Party as the leader and teacher of the people; he called for the presentation of all the most important questions before the opinion of knowledgeable workers, before the opinion of their party; he said: 'We believe in it, we see in it the wisdom, the honour, and the conscience of our epoch'.

Lenin resolutely stood against every attempt aimed at belittling or weakening the directing role of the party in the structure of the Soviet state. He worked out Bolshevik principles of party direction and norms of party life, stressing that the guiding principle of party leadership is its collegiality. Already during the pre-revolutionary years Lenin called the Central Committee of the party a collective of leaders and the guardian and interpreter of party principles. 'In the period between congresses', pointed out Lenin, 'the Central Committee guards and interprets the principles of the party'.

Underlining the role of the Central Committee of the party and its authority, Vladimir Ilyich pointed out: 'Our Central Committee constituted itself as a closely centralized and highly authoritative group. . . . '

During Lenin's life the Central Committee of the party was a real expression of collective leadership of the party and of the nation. Being a militant Marxist-revolutionist, always unyielding in matters of principle, Lenin never imposed by force his views upon his co-workers. He tried to convince; he patiently explained his opinions to others. Lenin always diligently observed that the norms of party life were realized, that the Party Rules were enforced, that party congresses and the plenary sessions of the Central Committee took place at the proper intervals.[1]

In addition to the great accomplishments of V. I. Lenin for the victory of the working class and of the working peasants, for the victory of our party and for the application of the ideas of scientific communism to life, his acute mind expressed itself also in the fact that he detected in Stalin in time those negative characteristics which resulted later in grave consequences. Fearing for the future fate of the party and of the Soviet nation, V. I. Lenin made a completely correct characterization of Stalin, pointing out that it was necessary to consider the question of transferring Stalin from the position of the Secretary General because of the fact that Stalin was excessively rude, that he did not have a proper attitude towards his comrades, that he was capricious and abused his power.

In December 1922 in a letter to the party congress Vladimir Ilyich wrote:

> After taking over the position of Secretary General Comrade Stalin accumulated in his hands immeasurable power and I am not certain whether he will be always able to use this power with the required care.

This letter — a political document of tremendous importance, known in the party history as Lenin's 'testament' — has been distributed to the delegates to the 20th Party Congress. You have read it, and will undoubtedly read it again more than once. You might reflect on Lenin's plain words, in which expression is given to Vladimir Ilyich's anxiety concerning the party, the people, the state, and the future direction of party policy.

Vladimir Ilyich said:

> Stalin is excessively rude, and this defect, which can be freely tolerated in our midst and in contacts among us Communists, becomes intolerable in one holding the position of Secretary General. Because of this, I propose that comrades think over a method of removing Stalin from this position and appointing another man to it, someone who, in all respects, would differ from Stalin in having only one advantage, namely, greater tolerance, greater loyalty, greater kindness and a more considerate attitude towards comrades, less capriciousness, etc.

This document of Lenin's was made known to the delegates at the 13th Party Congress, who discussed the question of transferring Stalin from the position of Secretary General. The delegates declared themselves in favour of retaining Stalin in this post, hoping that he would heed the critical remarks of Vladimir Ilyich and would be able to overcome the defects which caused Lenin serious anxiety.

Comrades! The party congress should acquaint itself with two new documents, which confirm Stalin's character as already outlined by Vladimir Ilyich Lenin in his 'testament'. These documents are a letter from Nadezhda Konstantinovna Krupskaya [Lenin's wife] to Kamenev, who was at that time head of the Political Bureau, and a personal letter from Vladimir Ilyich Lenin to Stalin.

I will now read these documents:

Lev Borisovich!

Because of a short letter which I had written in words dictated to me by Vladimir Ilyich by permission of the doctors, Stalin allowed himself yesterday an unusually rude outburst directed at me. This is not my first day in the party. During all these thirty years I have never heard from any comrade one word of rudeness. The business of the party and of Ilyich are not less dear to me than to Stalin. I need at present the maximum of self-control. What one can and what one cannot discuss with Ilyich, I know better than any doctor, because I know what makes him nervous and what does not, in any case I know better than Stalin. I am turning to you and to Grigory [i.e. Zinoviev] as to much closer comrades of V. I. and I beg you to protect me from rude interference with my private life and from vile invectives and threats. I have no doubt as to what will be the unanimous decision of the Control Commission, with which Stalin sees fit to threaten me, but I have neither the strength nor the time to waste on this foolish quarrel. And I am a living person and my nerves are strained to the utmost.

N. KRUPSKAYA

Nadezhda Konstantinovna wrote this letter on December 23, 1922. After two and a half months, in March 1923, Vladimir Ilyich Lenin sent Stalin the following letter:

To Comrade Stalin
Copies for: Kamenev and Zinoviev
Dear Comrade Stalin!
You had the rudeness to summon my wife to the telephone and to abuse her. Despite the fact that she told you that

she agreed to forget what was said, nevertheless Zinoviev and Kamenev heard about it from her. I have no intention to forget so easily what is being done against me, and I need not stress here that I consider as directed against me that which is being done against my wife. I ask you, therefore, that you weigh carefully whether you are agreeable to retracting your words and apologizing or whether you prefer the severance of relations between us. *(Commotion in the hall.)*

Sincerely,
LENIN

March 5, 1923[2]

Comrades! I will not comment on these documents.[3] They speak eloquently for themselves. Since Stalin could behave in this manner during Lenin's life, could behave thus toward Nadezhda Konstantinovna Krupskaya, whom the party knows well and values highly as a loyal friend of Lenin and as an active fighter for the cause of the party since its creation — we can easily imagine how Stalin treated other people. These negative characteristics of his developed steadily and during the last years acquired an absolutely insufferable character.

As later events have proven, Lenin's anxiety was justified: in the first period after Lenin's death Stalin still paid attention to his [i.e., Lenin's] advice, but later he began to disregard the serious admonitions of Vladimir Ilyich.

When we analyze the practice of Stalin in regard to the direction of the party and of the country, when we pause to consider everything which Stalin perpetrated, we must be convinced that Lenin's fears were justified. The negative characteristics of Stalin, which, in Lenin's time, were only incipient, transformed themselves during the last years into a grave abuse of power by Stalin, which caused untold harm to our party.

We have to consider this matter seriously and analyze it correctly in order that we may preclude any possibility of a repetition in any form whatever of what took place during the life of Stalin, who absolutely did not tolerate collegiality in leadership and in work, and who practiced brutal violence, not only toward everything which opposed him, but also toward that which seemed, to his capricious and despotic character, contrary to his concepts.

28

Stalin acted not through persuasion, explanation, and patient co-operation with people, but by imposing his concepts and demanding absolute submission to his opinion. Whoever opposed this concept or tried to prove his viewpoint, and the correctness of his position, was doomed to removal from the leading collective and to subsequent moral and physical annihilation. This was especially true during the period following the 17th Party Congress [in 1934], when many prominent party leaders and rank-and-file party workers, honest and dedicated to the cause of communism, fell victim to Stalin's despotism.

We must affirm that the party fought a serious fight against the Trotskyites, rightists and bourgeois nationalists, and that it disarmed ideologically all the enemies of Leninism. This ideological fight was carried on successfully, as a result of which the party became strengthened and tempered. Here Stalin played a positive role.

The party conducted a great political ideological struggle against those in its own ranks who proposed anti-Leninist theses, who represented a political line hostile to the party and to the cause of socialism. This was a stubborn and a difficult fight but a necessary one, because the political line of both the Trotskyite-Zinovievite bloc and of the Bukharinites led actually toward the restoration of capitalism and capitulation to the world bourgeoisie. Let us consider for a moment what would have happened if in 1928-1929 the political line of right deviation had prevailed among us, or orientation toward 'cotton-dress industrialization', or toward the kulak, etc.[4] We would not now have a powerful heavy industry, we would not have the kolkhozes, we would find ourselves disarmed and weak in a capitalist encirclement.

It was for this reason that the party led an inexorable ideological fight and explained to all party members and to the non-party masses the harm and the danger of the anti-Leninist proposals of the Trotskyite opposition and the rightist opportunists. And this great work of explaining the party line bore fruit; both the Trotskyites and the rightist opportunists were politically isolated; the overwhelming party majority supported the Leninist line and the party was able to awaken and organize the working masses to apply the Leninist party line and to build socialism.

Worth noting is the fact that even in the course of the furious ideological fight against the Trotskyites, the Zinovievites, the Bukharinites and others, extreme repressive measures were not used against them. The fight was on ideological grounds. But some years later when socialism in our country was fundamentally constructed, when the exploiting classes were generally liquidated, when the Soviet social structure had radically changed, when the social basis for political movements and groups hostile to the party had violently contracted, when the ideological opponents of the party were long since defeated politically — then the repression directed against them began.

It was precisely during this period (1935-1937-1938) that the practice of mass repression through the government apparatus was born, first against the enemies of Leninism — Trotskyites, Zinovievites, Bukharinites, long since politically defeated by the party, and subsequently also against many honest communists, against those party cadres who had borne the heavy load of the Civil War and the first and most difficult years of industrialization and collectivization, who actively fought against the Trotskyites and the rightists for the Leninist party line.

Stalin originated the concept 'enemy of the people'. This term automatically rendered it unnecessary that the ideological errors of a man or men engaged in a controversy be proven; this term made possible the employment of the most cruel repression, violating all norms of revolutionary legality, against anyone who in any way disagreed with Stalin, against those who were only suspected of hostile intent, against those who had bad reputations. This concept, 'enemy of the people', actually eliminated the possibility of any kind of ideological struggle or the making of one's views known on this or that issue, even those of a practical character. In the main, and in actuality, the only proof of guilt used, against all norms of current legal science, was the 'confession' of the accused himself; and, as subsequent probing proved, 'confessions' were acquired through physical pressures against the accused.

This led to glaring violations of revolutionary legality, and to the fact that many entirely innocent persons, who in the past had defended the party line, became victims.

We must assert that in regard to those persons who in their time had opposed the party line, there were often no sufficiently serious reasons for their physical annihilation. The formula, 'enemy of the people', was specifically introduced for the purpose of physically annihilating such individuals.

It is a fact that many persons, who were later annihilated as enemies of the party and people, had worked with Lenin during his life. Some of these persons had made errors during Lenin's life, but, despite this, Lenin benefited by their work, he corrected them and he did everything possible to retain them in the ranks of the party; he induced them to follow him.

In this connection the delegates to the party congress should familiarize themselves with an unpublished note by V. I. Lenin directed to the Central Committee's Political Bureau in October 1920. Outlining the duties of the Control Commission, Lenin wrote that the Commission should be transformed into a real 'organ of party and proletarian conscience'.

> As a special task of the Control Commission there is recommended a considerate, individualized attitude towards, and often even a type of therapy for, the representatives of the so-called opposition — those who have experienced a psychological crisis because of failure in their soviet or party career. An effort should be made to reassure them, to explain the matter to them in a comradely fashion, to find for them (avoiding the method of issuing orders) a job for which they are psychologically fitted. Advice and rules relating to this matter are to be formulated by the Central Committee's Organizational Bureau, etc.

Everyone knows how irreconcilable Lenin was with the ideological enemies of Marxism, with those who deviated from the correct party line. At the same time, however, Lenin, as is apparent from the present document, in his practice of directing the party demanded the most intimate party contact with people who had shown indecision or temporary unconformity with the party line, but whom it was possible to return to the party path. Lenin advised that such people should be patiently educated without the application of extreme methods.

Lenin's wisdom in dealing with people was evident in his work with cadres.

An entirely different relationship with people characterized Stalin. Lenin's traits — patient work with people; stubborn and painstaking education of them; the ability to induce people to follow him without using compulsion, but rather through the ideological influence on them of the whole collective — were entirely foreign to Stalin. He [Stalin] discarded the Leninist method of convincing and educating; he abandoned the method

31

of ideological struggle for that of administrative violence, mass repressions, and terror. He acted on an increasingly larger scale and more stubbornly through punitive organs, at the same time often violating all existing norms of morality and of Soviet laws.

Arbitrary behavior by one person encouraged and permitted arbitrariness in others. Mass arrests and deportations of many thousands of people, execution without trial and without normal investigation created conditions of insecurity, fear and even desperation.

This, of course, did not contribute toward unity of the party ranks and of all strata of working people, but on the contrary brought about the annihilation and expulsion from the party of workers who were loyal but inconvenient to Stalin.

Our party fought for the implementation of Lenin's plans for the construction of socialism. This was an ideological fight. Had Leninist principles been observed during the course of this fight, had the party's devotion to principles been skilfully combined with a keen and solicitous concern for people, had they not been repelled and wasted but rather drawn to our side — we certainly would not have had such a brutal violation of revolutionary legality and many thousands of people would not have fallen victim of the method of terror. Extraordinary methods would then have been resorted to only against those people who had in fact committed criminal acts against the Soviet system.

Let us recall some historical facts.

In the days before the October Revolution two members of the Central Committee of the Bolshevik Party — Kamenev and Zinoviev — declared themselves against Lenin's plan for an armed uprising. In addition, on October 18 they published in the Menshevik newspaper, *Novaia Zhizn'*, a statement declaring that the Bolsheviks were making preparations for an uprising and that they considered it adventuristic. Kamenev and Zinoviev thus disclosed to the enemy the decision of the Central Committee to stage the uprising, and that the uprising had been organized to take place within the very near future.

This was treason against the party and against the revolution. In this connection, V. I. Lenin wrote: 'Kamenev and Zinoviev revealed the decision of the Central Committee of their Party on the armed uprising to Rodzyanko and Kerensky . . . ' He put before the Central Committee the question of Zinoviev's and Kamenev's expulsion from the party.[5]

However, after the Great Socialist October Revolution, as it is known, Zinoviev and Kamenev were given leading positions. Lenin put them in positions in which they carried out most responsible party tasks and participated actively in the work of the leading party and soviet organs. It is known that Zinoviev and Kamenev committed a number of other serious errors during Lenin's life. In his 'testament' Lenin warned that 'Zinoviev's and Kamenev's October episode was of course not an accident'. But Lenin did not pose the question of their arrest and certainly not their shooting.

Or let us take the example of the Trotskyites. At present, after a sufficiently long historical period, we can speak about the fight with the Trotskyites with complete calm and can analyze this matter with sufficient objectivity. After all, around Trotsky there were people whose origin cannot by any means be traced to bourgeois society. Part of them belonged to the party intelligentsia and a certain part were recruited from among the workers. We can name many individuals who in their time joined the Trotskyites; however, these same individuals took an active part in the workers' movement before the revolution, during the Socialist October Revolution itself, and also in the consolidation of the victory of this greatest of revolutions. Many of them broke with Trotskyism and returned to Leninist positions. Was it necessary to annihilate such people? We are deeply convinced that had Lenin lived such an extreme method would not have been used against many of them.

Such are only a few historical facts. But can it be said that Lenin did not decide to use even the most severe means against enemies of the revolution when this was actually necessary? No, no one can say this. Vladimir Ilyich demanded uncompromising dealings with the enemies of the revolution and of the working class and when necessary resorted ruthlessly to such methods. You will recall only V. I. Lenin's fight with the Socialist Revolutionary organizers of the anti-Soviet uprising, with the counter-revolutionary kulaks in 1918 and with others, when Lenin without hesitation used the most extreme methods against the enemies. Lenin used such methods, however, only against actual class enemies and not against those who blunder, who err, and whom it was possible to lead through ideological influence, and even retain in the leadership.

Lenin used severe methods only in the most necessary cases,

33

c

when the exploiting classes were still in existence and were vigorously opposing the revolution, when the struggle for survival was decidedly assuming the sharpest forms, even including a civil war.

Stalin, on the other hand, used extreme methods and mass repressions at a time when the revolution was already victorious, when the Soviet state was strengthened, when the exploiting classes were already liquidated and socialist relations were rooted solidly in all phases of the national economy, when our party was politically consolidated and had strengthened itself both numerically and ideologically. It is clear that here Stalin showed in a whole series of cases his intolerance, his brutality and his abuse of power. Instead of proving his political correctness and mobilizing the masses, he often chose the path of repression and physical annihilation, not only against actual enemies, but also against individuals who had not committed any crimes against the party and the Soviet government. Here we see no wisdom but only a demonstration of the brutal force which had once so alarmed V. I. Lenin.

Lately, especially after the unmasking of the Beria gang, the Central Committee has looked into a number of cases fabricated by this gang. This revealed a very ugly picture of brutal willfulness connected with the incorrect behavior of Stalin. As facts prove, Stalin, using his unlimited power, allowed himself many abuses, acting in the name of the Central Committee without asking for the opinion of the Committee members or even of the members of the Central Committee's Political Bureau; often he did not inform them about his personal decisions concerning very important party and government matters.[6]

In considering the question of the cult of the individual we must first of all show everyone what harm this caused to the interests of our party.

Vladimir Ilyich Lenin always stressed the party's role and significance in the direction of the socialist government of workers and peasants; he saw in this the chief precondition for a successful building of socialism in our country. Pointing to the great responsibility of the Bolshevik Party, as the ruling party in the Soviet state, Lenin called for the most meticulous observance of all norms of party life; he called for the realization of the principles of collegiality in the direction of the party and the state.

34

Collegiality of leadership flows from the very nature of our party, a party built on the principles of democratic centralism. 'This means', said Lenin,

> that all party matters are accomplished by all party members — directly or through representatives — who without any exceptions are subject to the same rules; in addition, all administrative members, all directing collegia, all holders of party positions are elective, they must account for their activities and are recallable.

It is known that Lenin himself offered an example of the most careful observance of these principles. There was no matter so important that Lenin himself decided it without asking for advice and approval of the majority of the Central Committee members or of the members of the Central Committee's Political Bureau.

In the most difficult period for our party and our country, Lenin considered it necessary regularly to convoke congresses, party conferences, and plenary sessions of the Central Committee at which all the most important questions were discussed and where resolutions carefully worked out by the collective of leaders were approved.

We can recall, for an example, the year 1918 when the country was threatened by the attack of the imperialist interventionists. In this situation the 7th Party Congress was convened in order to discuss a vitally important matter which could not be postponed — the matter of peace. In 1919, while the Civil War was raging, the 8th Party Congress convened, which adopted a new party program, decided such important matters as the relationship with the peasant masses, the organization of the Red Army, the leading role of the party in the work of the soviets, the correction of the social composition of the party, and other matters. In 1920 the 9th Party Congress was convened which laid down guiding principles pertaining to the party's work in the sphere of economic construction. In 1921, the 10th Party Congress accepted Lenin's New Economic Policy and the historical resolution called 'On Party Unity'.

During Lenin's life party congresses were convened regularly; always, when a radical turn in the development of the party and the country took place, Lenin considered it absolutely necessary that the party discuss at length all the basic matters pertaining to internal and foreign policy and to questions bearing on the development of party and government.

It is very characteristic that Lenin addressed to the party congress as the highest party organ his last articles, letters and remarks. During the period between congresses the Central Committee of the party, acting as the most authoritative leading collective, meticulously observed the principles of the party and carried out its policy.

So it was during Lenin's life.

Were our party's sacred Leninist principles observed after the death of Vladimir Ilyich?

Whereas during the first few years after Lenin's death party congresses and Central Committee plenums took place more or less regularly, later, when Stalin began increasingly to abuse his power, these principles were crudely violated. This was especially evident during the last 15 years of his life. Was it a normal situation when over 13 years elapsed between the 18th and 19th Party Congresses, years during which our party and our country experienced so many important events? These events demanded categorically that the party pass resolutions pertaining to the country's defense during the Patriotic War and to peacetime construction after the war. Even after the end of the war a congress was not convened for over 7 years.

Central Committee plenums were hardly ever called. It should be sufficient to mention that during all the years of the Patriotic War not a single Central Committee plenum took place.[7] It is true that there was an attempt to call a Central Committee plenum in October 1941, when Central Committee members from the whole country were called to Moscow. They waited two days for the opening of the plenum, but in vain. Stalin did not even want to meet and to talk to the Central Committee members. This fact shows how demoralized Stalin was in the first months of the war and how haughtily and disdainfully he treated the Central Committee members.

In practice Stalin ignored the norms of party life and trampled on the Leninist principle of collective party leadership.

Stalin's arbitrariness *vis-à-vis* the party and its Central Committee became fully evident after the 17th Party Congress which took place in 1934.

Having at its disposal numerous data showing brutal arbitrariness toward party cadres, the Central Committee has created a

36

party commission under the control of the Central Committee Presidium; it was charged with investigating what made possible the mass repressions against the majority of the Central Committee members and candidates elected at the 17th Congress of the All-Union Communist Party (Bolsheviks).

The Commission has acquainted itself with a large quantity of materials in the NKVD archives and with other documents and has established many facts pertaining to the fabrication of cases against communists, to false accusations, to glaring abuses of socialist legality — which resulted in the death of innocent people. It became apparent that many party, soviet and economic activists who were branded in 1937-1938 as 'enemies' were actually never enemies, spies, wreckers, etc., but were always honest communists; they were only so stigmatized, and often, no longer able to bear barbaric tortures, they charged themselves (at the order of the investigative judges — the falsifiers) with all kinds of grave and unlikely crimes. The Commission has presented to the Central Committee Presidium lengthy and documented materials pertaining to mass repressions against the delegates to the 17th Party Congress and against members of the Central Committee elected at that congress. These materials have been studied by the Presidium of the Central Committee.

It has been established that of the 139 members and candidates of the Party's Central Committee who were elected at the 17th Congress, 98 persons, i.e. 70 percent, were arrested and shot (mostly in 1937-1938). (*Indignation in the hall.*)

What was the composition of the delegates to the 17th Congress? It is known that 80 percent of the voting participants of the 17th Congress joined the party during the years of conspiracy before the Revolution and during the Civil War; this means before 1921. By social origin the basic mass of the delegates to the congress were workers (60 percent of the voting members).

For this reason, it was inconceivable that a congress so composed would have elected a Central Committee, a majority of which would prove to be enemies of the party. The only reason why 70 percent of the Central Committee members and candidates elected at the 17th Congress were branded as enemies of the party and of the people was that honest communists were slandered, accusations against them were fabricated, and revolutionary legality was gravely undermined.

The same fate met not only the Central Committee members

37

but also the majority of the delegates to the 17th Party Congress. Of 1,966 delegates with either voting or advisory rights, 1,108 persons were arrested on charges of counter-revolutionary crimes, i.e., decidedly more than a majority. This very fact shows how absurd, wild and contrary to common sense were the charges of counter-revolutionary crimes made out, as we now see, against the majority of participants at the 17th Party Congress. (*Indignation in the hall*.) .

We should recall that the 17th Party Congress is historically known as the Congress of Victors. The delegates to the congress were active participants in the building of our socialist state; many of them suffered and fought for party interests during the pre-revolutionary years in the conspiracy and at the Civil War fronts; they fought their enemies valiantly and often looked unflinchingly into the face of death. How then can we believe that such people could prove to be 'two-faced' and join the camps of the enemies of socialism during the era after the political liquidation of Zinovievites, Trotskyites and rightists and after the great accomplishments of socialist construction?

This was the result of the abuse of power by Stalin, who began to use mass terror against party cadres.[8]

What is the reason that mass repressions against activists increased more and more after the 17th Party Congress? It was because at that time Stalin had so elevated himself above the party and above the nation that he ceased to consider either the Central Committee or the party. While he still reckoned with the opinion of the collective before the 17th Congress, after the complete political liquidation of the Trotskyites, Zinovievites and Bukharinites, when as a result of that fight and socialist victories the party achieved unity, Stalin ceased to an ever greater degree to consider the members of the Party's Central Committee and even the members of the Political Bureau. Stalin thought that now he could decide all things alone and all he needed were statisticians;[9] he treated all others in such a way that they could only listen to and praise him.

After the criminal murder of S. M. Kirov[10] mass repressions and brutal acts of violation of socialist legality began. On the evening of December 1, 1934, on Stalin's initiative (without the approval of the Political Bureau — which was passed two days later, casually) the secretary of the Presidium of the Central Executive Committee, Yenukidze, signed the following directive.

I. Investigative agencies are directed to speed up the cases of those accused of the preparation or execution of acts of terror.

II. Judicial organs are directed not to hold up the execution of death sentences pertaining to crimes of this category in order to consider the possibility of pardon, because the Presidium of the Central Executive Committee [of the] U.S.S.R. does not consider as possible the receiving of petitions of this sort.

III. The organs of the Commissariat for Internal Affairs [NKVD] are directed to execute death sentences against criminals of the above-mentioned category immediately after the passage of sentences.

This directive became the basis for mass acts of abuse against socialist legality. During many of the fabricated court cases the accused were charged with 'the preparation' of terroristic acts; this deprived them of any possibility that their cases might be re-examined, even when they stated before the court that their 'confessions' were secured by force, and when, in a convincing manner, they disproved the accusations against them.

It must be asserted that to this day the circumstances surrounding Kirov's murder hide many things which are inexplicable and mysterious and demand most careful examination. There are reasons for the suspicion that the killer of Kirov, Nikolaev, was assisted by someone from among the people whose duty it was to protect the person of Kirov. A month and a half before the killing, Nikolaev was arrested on the grounds of suspicious behavior, but he was released and not even searched. It is an unusually suspicious circumstance that when the Chekist[11] assigned to protect Kirov was being brought for an interrogation, on December 2, 1934, he was killed in a car 'accident' in which no other occupants of the car were harmed. After the murder of Kirov, top functionaries of the Leningrad NKVD were given very light sentences, but in 1937 they were shot. We can assume that they were shot in order to cover the traces of the organizers of Kirov's killing. (*Movement in the hall.*)

Mass repressions grew tremendously from the end of 1936[12] after a telegram from Stalin and Zhdanov, dated from Sochi on September 25, 1936, was addressed to Kaganovich, Molotov and other members of the Political Bureau. The content of the telegram was as follows:

> We deem it absolutely necessary and urgent that Comrade Yezhov be nominated to the post of People's Commissar for Internal Affairs. Yagoda has definitely proved himself to be incapable of unmasking the Trotskyite-Zinovievite bloc. The OGPU is 4 years behind in this matter. This is noted by all party workers and by the majority of the representatives of the NKVD.

Strictly speaking we should stress that Stalin did not meet with and therefore could not know the opinion of party workers.

This Stalinist formulation that the 'NKVD is 4 years behind' in applying mass repression and that there is a necessity for 'catching up' with the neglected work directly pushed the NKVD workers on the path of mass arrests and executions.

We should state that this formulation was also forced on the February-March plenary session of the Central Committee of the All-Union Communist Party (Bolsheviks) in 1937. The plenary resolution approved it on the basis of Yezhov's report, 'Lessons flowing from the harmful activity, diversion and espionage of the Japanese-German-Trotskyite agents', stating:

> The Plenary Session of the Central Committee of the All-Union Communist Party (Bolsheviks) considers that all facts revealed during the investigation into the matter of the anti-Soviet Trotskyite center and of its followers in the provinces show that the People's Commissariat for Internal Affairs has fallen behind at least 4 years in the attempt to unmask these most inexorable enemies of the people.

The mass repressions at this time were made under the slogan of a fight against the Trotskyites. Did the Trotskyites at this time actually constitute such a danger to our party and to the Soviet state? We should recall that in 1927 on the eve of the 15th Party Congress only some 4,000 votes were cast for the Trotskyite-Zinovievite opposition, while there were 724,000 for the party line. During the 10 years which passed between the 15th Party Congress and the February-March Central Committee Plenum Trotskyism was completely disarmed; many former Trotskyites had changed their former views and worked in the various sectors building socialism. It is clear that in the situation of socialist victory there was no basis for mass terror in the country.

Stalin's report at the February-March plenary session of the Central Committee in 1937, 'Deficiencies of Party work and methods for the liquidation of the Trotskyites and of other double-dealers' contained an attempt at theoretical justification of the mass terror policy under the pretext that as we march forward toward socialism, class war must allegedly sharpen. Stalin asserted that both history and Lenin taught him this.

Actually Lenin taught that the application of revolutionary violence is necessitated by the resistance of the exploiting classes, and this referred to the era when the exploiting classes existed and were powerful. As soon as the nation's political situation had improved, when in January 1920 the Red Army took Rostov and thus won a most important victory over Denikin, Lenin instructed Dzerzhinsky [Chief of the Cheka] to stop mass terror and to abolish the death penalty. Lenin justified this important political move of the Soviet state in the following manner in his report at the session of the All-Russian Central Executive Committee on February 2, 1920:

> Terror was imposed on us by the terrorism of the Entente, when mighty world powers threw their hordes against us, stopping at nothing. We would not have lasted two days had we not answered these attempts of officers and White Guardists in a merciless fashion; this meant [the use of] terror, but this was forced upon us by the terrorist methods of the Entente, and as soon as we attained a decisive victory, even before the end of the war, immediately after taking Rostov, we gave up the use of the death penalty and thus proved that our attitude to our own program was just as we had promised. We say that the application of violence issues from the decision to crush the exploiters, the big landowners and the capitalists; as soon as this is accomplished we give up the use of all extraordinary methods. We have proved this in practice.

Stalin deviated from these clear and plain precepts of Lenin. Stalin put the party and the NKVD up to the use of mass terror when the exploiting classes had been liquidated in our country and when there were no serious reasons for the use of extraordinary mass terror.

This terror was actually directed not at the remnants of the exploiting classes but against honest workers of the party and of the Soviet state; against them were made lying, slanderous and

41

absurd accusations concerning 'two-facedness', 'espionage', 'sabotage', preparation of fictitious 'plots', etc.

At the February-March Plenary Session of the Central Committee in 1937 many members actually questioned the rightness of the established course regarding mass repressions under the pretext of combating 'two-facedness'.

Comrade Postyshev[13] most ably expressed these doubts. He said:

> I have philosophized that the severe years of fighting have passed; party members who have lost their backbones have broken down or have joined the camp of the enemy; the healthy elements have fought for the party. These were the years of industrialization and collectivization. I never thought it possible that after this severe era had passed Karpov and people like him would find themselves in the camp of the enemy. (Karpov was a worker in the Ukrainian Central Committee whom Postyshev knew well.) And now, according to the testimony, it appears that Karpov was recruited in 1934 by the Trotskyites. I personally do not believe that in 1934 an honest party member who had trod the long road of unrelenting fight against enemies, for the party and for socialism, would now be in the camp of the enemies. I do not believe it . . . I cannot imagine how it would be possible to travel with the party during the difficult years and then, in 1934, join the Trotskyites. It is an odd thing . . . (*Movement in the hall.*)

Using Stalin's formulation, namely that the closer we are to socialism, the more enemies we will have, and using the resolution of the February-March Central Committee plenum passed on the basis of Yezhov's report — the provocateurs who had infiltrated the state security organs together with conscienceless careerists began to defend in the name of the party the mass terror against party cadres, cadres of the Soviet state and the ordinary Soviet citizens. It should suffice to say that the number of arrests based on charges of counter-revolutionary crimes grew tenfold between 1936 and 1937.

It is known that brutal willfulness was practiced against leading party workers. The Party Rules approved at the 17th Party Congress were based on the Leninist principles expressed at the 10th Party Congress. They stated that in order to apply an extreme method such as exclusion from the party against a Central Committee member, against a Central Committee candidate, or against a member of the Party Control Commission, 'it is necessary to call a plenary session of the Central Committee and to invite to the session all Central Committee candidate members and all members of the Party Control Commission'; only if two thirds of the members of such a general assembly of responsible party leaders find it necessary, only then can a Central Committee member or candidate be expelled.

The majority of the Central Committee members and candidates elected at the 17th Congress and arrested in 1937-1938 were expelled from the party illegally through the crude abuse of the Party Rules, because the question of their expulsion was never studied at a plenary session of the Central Committee.

Now when the cases of some of these so-called 'spies' and 'saboteurs' were examined it was found that all their cases were fabricated. Confessions of guilt of many arrested and charged with enemy activity were gained with the help of cruel and inhuman tortures.

At the same time Stalin, as we have been informed by members of the Political Bureau of that time, did not show them the statements of many accused political activists when they retracted their confessions before the military tribunal and asked for an objective examination of their cases. There were many such declarations, and Stalin doubtlessly knew of them.

The Central Committee considers it absolutely necessary to inform the Congress of many fabricated 'cases' against the members of the party's Central Committee elected at the 17th Party Congress.

An example of vile provocation, of odious falsification and of criminal violation of revolutionary legality is the case of the former candidate for the Central Committee Political Bureau, one of the most eminent workers of the party and of the Soviet government, Comrade Eikhe,[14] who was a party member since 1905. (*Commotion in the hall.*)

Comrade Eikhe was arrested on April 29, 1938 on the basis of slanderous materials, without the sanction of the Prosecutor of the U.S.S.R., which was finally received 15 months after the arrest.

Investigation of Eikhe's case was made in a manner which

most brutally violated Soviet legality and was accompanied by willfulness and falsification.

Eikhe was forced under torture to sign in advance a protocol of his confession prepared by the investigating judges, in which he and several other eminent party workers were accused of anti-Soviet activity.

On October 1, 1939, Eikhe sent his statement to Stalin in which he categorically denied his guilt and asked for an examination of his case. In the statement he wrote: 'There is no more bitter misery than to sit in the jail of a government for which I have always fought'.

A second declaration of Eikhe has been preserved which he sent to Stalin on October 27, 1939; in it he cited facts very convincingly and countered the slanderous accusations made against him, arguing that this provocatory accusation was on the one hand the work of real Trotskyites whose arrests he had sanctioned as First Secretary of the West Siberian Krai Party Committee and who conspired in order to take revenge on him, and, on the other hand, the result of the base falsification of materials by the investigating judges.

Eikhe wrote in his declaration:

> . . . On October 25 of this year I was informed that the investigation in my case had been concluded and I was given access to the materials of this investigation. Had I been guilty of only one hundredth of the crimes with which I am charged, I would not have dared to send you this pre-execution declaration; however, I have not been guilty of even one of the things with which I am charged and my heart is clean of even the shadow of baseness. I have never in my life told you a word of falsehood and now, finding my two feet in the grave, I am also not lying. My whole case is a typical example of provocation, slander and violation of the elementary basis of revolutionary legality . . .
>
> . . . The confessions which were made part of my file are not only absurd but contain some slander toward the Central Committee of the All-Union Communist Party (Bolsheviks) and toward the Council of People's Commissars because correct resolutions of the Central Committee of the All-Union Communist Party (Bolsheviks) and of the Council of People's Commissars which were not made on

my initiative and [were made] without my participation are presented as hostile acts of counter-revolutionary organizations made at my suggestion . . .

I am now alluding to the most disgraceful part of my life and to my really grave guilt against the party and against you. This is my confession of counter-revolutionary activity . . . The case is as follows: not being able to suffer the tortures to which I was submitted by Ushakov and Nikolaev — and especially by the former — who utilized the knowledge that my broken ribs had not properly mended and were causing me great pain — I was forced to accuse myself and others.

The majority of my confession was suggested or dictated by Ushakov, and the remainder is my reconstruction of NKVD materials from Western Siberia for which I assumed all responsibility. If any part of the story which Ushakov fabricated and which I signed did not properly hang together, I was forced to sign another variation. The same thing was done to Rukhimovich, who was at first designated as a member of the reserve net and whose name later was removed without telling me anything about it; the same was also done with the leader of the reserve net, supposedly created by Bukharin in 1935. At first I wrote my name in, and then I was instructed to insert Mezhlauk. There were other similar incidents.

. . . I am asking and begging you that you again examine my case and this not for the purpose of sparing me but in order to unmask the vile provocation which has wound itself like a snake around many persons in a great degree due to my meanness and criminal slander. I have never betrayed you or the party. I know that I perish because of vile and mean work of the enemies of the party and of the people, who fabricated the provocation against me.

It would appear that such an important declaration was worth an examination by the Central Committee. This, however, was not done and the declaration was transmitted to Beria while the terrible maltreatment of the Political Bureau candidate, Comrade Eikhe, continued.

On February 2, 1940 Eikhe was brought before the court. Here he did not confess any guilt and spoke as follows:

45

In all the so-called confessions of mine there is not one letter written by me with the exception of my signatures under the protocols which were forced from me. I made my confession under pressure from the investigating judge who from the time of my arrest tormented me. After that I began to write all this nonsense . . . The most important thing for me is to tell the court, the party and Stalin that I am not guilty. I have never been guilty of any conspiracy. I will die believing in the truth of party policy as I have believed in it during my whole life.

On February 4 Eikhe was shot. (*Indignation in the hall.*) It has been definitely established now that Eikhe's case was fabricated; he has been posthumously rehabilitated.

Comrade Rudzutak,[15] candidate member of the Political Bureau, member of the party since 1905, who spent 10 years in a tsarist hard labor camp, completely retracted in court the confession which was forced from him. The protocol of the session of the Military Collegium of the Supreme Court[16] contains the following statement by Rudzutak:

> . . . The only plea which he places before the Court is that the Central Committee of the All-Union Communist Party (Bolsheviks) be informed that there is in the NKVD an as yet not liquidated center which is craftily manufacturing cases, and which forces innocent persons to confess; there is no opportunity to prove one's nonparticipation in crimes to which the confessions of various persons testify. The investigating methods are such that they force people to lie and slander entirely innocent persons in addition to those who already stand accused. He asks the Court that he be allowed to inform the Central Committee of the All-Union Communist Party (Bolsheviks) about all this in writing. He assures the Court that he personally has never had any evil designs in regard to the policy of our party because he has always agreed with the party policy pertaining to all spheres of economic and cultural activity.

This declaration of Rudzutak was ignored, despite the fact that Rudzutak was in his time the chief of the Central Control Commission which was called into being in accordance with Lenin's concept for the purpose of fighting for party unity . . . In this manner fell the chief of this highly authoritative party organ, a victim of brutal willfulness: he was not even called before the Central Committee's Political Bureau because Stalin did not want to talk to him. Sentence was pronounced on him in 20 minutes and he was shot. (*Indignation in the hall.*)

After careful examination of the case in 1955 it was established that the accusation against Rudzutak was false and that it was based on slanderous materials. Rudzutak has been rehabilitated posthumously.

The way in which the former NKVD workers manufactured various fictitious 'anti-Soviet centers' and 'blocs' with the help of provocatory methods is seen from the confession of Comrade Rozenblum, party member since 1906, who was arrested in 1937 by the Leningrad NKVD.

During the examination in 1955 of the Komarov case Rozenblum revealed the following fact: when Rozenblum was arrested in 1937 he was subjected to terrible torture during which he was ordered to confess false information concerning himself and other persons. He was then brought to the office of Zakovsky, who offered him freedom on condition that he make before the Court a false confession fabricated in 1937 by the NKVD concerning 'sabotage, espionage and diversion in a terroristic center in Leningrad'. (*Movement in the hall.*) With unbelievable cynicism Zakovsky told about the vile 'mechanism' for the crafty creation of fabricated 'anti-Soviet plots'.

> In order to illustrate it to me [stated Rozenblum], Zakovsky gave me several possible variants of the organization of this center and of its branches. After he detailed the organization to me, Zakovsky told me that the NKVD would prepare the case of this center, remarking that the trial would be public.
>
> Before the court were to be brought 4 or 5 members of this center: Chudov, Ugarov, Smorodin, Pozern, Shaposhnikova (Chudov's wife) and others together with 2 or 3 members from the branches of this center . . .
>
> . . . The case of the Leningrad center has to be built solidly and for this reason witnesses are needed. Social origin (of course, in the past) and the party standing of the witness will play more than a small role.
>
> You, yourself [said Zakovsky], will not need to invent

anything. The NKVD will prepare for you a ready outline for every branch of the center; you will have to study it carefully and to remember well all questions and answers which the Court might ask. This case will be ready in 4-5 months, or perhaps a half year. During all this time you will be preparing yourself so that you will not compromise the investigation and yourself. Your future will depend on how the trial goes and on its results. If you begin to lie and to testify falsely, blame yourself. If you manage to endure it, you will save your head and we will feed and clothe you at the government's cost until your death.

This is the kind of vile thing which was then practiced. (*Movement in the hall.*)

Even more widely was the falsification of cases practiced in the provinces. The NKVD headquarters of the Sverdlov Oblast 'discovered' the so-called 'Ural uprising staff' — an organ of the bloc of rightists, Trotskyites, Socialist Revolutionaries, church leaders — whose chief supposedly was Secretary of the Sverdlov Oblast Party Committee and member of the Central Committee of the All-Union Communist Party (Bolsheviks), Kabakov, who had been a party member since 1914. The investigative materials of that time show that in almost all krais, oblasts and republics there allegedly existed 'rightist Trotskyite, espionage-terror and diversionary-sabotage organizations and centers' and that the heads of such organizations as a rule — for no known reason — were first secretaries of oblast or republic communist party committees or central committees. (*Movement in the hall.*)

Many thousands of honest and innocent communists died as a result of this monstrous falsification of such 'cases', as a result of the fact that all kinds of slanderous 'confessions' were accepted, and as a result of the practice of forcing accusations against oneself and others. In the same manner were fabricated the 'cases' against eminent party and state workers — Kosior, Chubar, Postyshev, Kosarev, and others.

In those years repressions on a mass scale were applied which were based on nothing tangible and which resulted in heavy cadre losses to the party.

The vicious practice was condoned of having the NKVD prepare lists of persons whose cases were under the jurisdiction of the Military Collegium of the Supreme Court and whose sentences were prepared in advance. Yezhov would send these lists to Stalin personally for his approval of the proposed punishment. In 1937-1938, 383 such lists containing the names of many thousands of party, soviet, komsomol, army and economic workers were sent to Stalin. He approved these lists.

A large proportion of these cases are being reviewed now and a great part of them are being voided because they were baseless and falsified. Suffice it to say that from 1954 to the present time the Military Collegium of the Supreme Court has rehabilitated 7,679 persons, many of whom were rehabilitated posthumously.

Mass arrests of party, soviet, economic and military workers caused tremendous harm to our country and to the cause of socialist advancement.

Mass repressions had a negative influence on the moral-political condition of the party, created a situation of uncertainty, contributed to the spreading of unhealthy suspicion, and sowed distrust among communists. All sorts of slanderers and careerists were active.

Resolutions of the January plenary session of the Central Committee, All-Union Communist Party (Bolsheviks), in 1938 brought some measure of improvement to the party organizations. However, widespread repression also existed in 1938.

Only because our party has at its disposal such great moral-political strength was it possible for it to survive the difficult events in 1937-1938 and to educate new cadres. There is, however, no doubt that our march forward toward socialism and toward the preparation of the country's defense would have been much more successful had it not been for the tremendous loss in cadres suffered as a result of the baseless and false mass repressions in 1937-1938.

We justly accuse Yezhov for the degenerate practices of 1937. But we have to answer these questions: Could Yezhov have arrested Kosior,[17] for instance, without the knowledge of Stalin? Was there an exchange of opinions or a Political Bureau decision concerning this? No, there was not, just as there was none regarding other cases of this type. Could Yezhov have decided such important matters as the fate of eminent party figures? No, it would be a display of naivete to consider this the work of Yezhov alone. It is clear that these matters were decided by Stalin, and that without his orders and his sanction Yezhov could not have done this.

D

We have examined the cases and have rehabilitated Kosior, Rudzutak, Postyshev, Kosarev and others. For what causes were they arrested and sentenced? The review of evidence shows that there was no reason for this. They, like many others, were arrested without the prosecutor's knowledge. In such a situation there is no need for any sanction, for what sort of a sanction could there be when Stalin decided everything? He was the chief prosecutor in these cases. Stalin not only agreed to, but on his own initiative issued, arrest orders. We must say this so that the delegates to the congress can clearly undertake and themselves assess this and draw the proper conclusions.

Facts prove that many abuses were made on Stalin's orders without reckoning with any norms of party and Soviet legality. Stalin was a very distrustful man, morbidly suspicious; we knew this from our work with him. He could look at a man and say: 'Why are your eyes so shifty today?' or 'Why are you turning so much today and avoiding looking me straight in the eyes?' The morbid suspicion created in him a general distrust even toward eminent party workers whom he had known for years. Everywhere and in everything he saw 'enemies', 'two-facers' and 'spies'.

Possessing unlimited power he indulged in great willfulness and choked a person morally and physically. A situation was created where one could not express one's own will.

When Stalin said that one or another should be arrested, it was necessary to accept on faith that he was an 'enemy of the people'. Meanwhile, Beria's gang, which ran the organs of state security, outdid itself in proving the guilt of the arrested and the truth of materials which it falsified. And what proofs were offered? The confessions of the arrested, and the investigating judges accepted these 'confessions'. And how is it possible that a person confesses to crimes which he has not committed? Only in one way — because of the application of physical methods of pressuring him, tortures, bringing him to a state of unconsciousness, deprivation of his judgment, taking away of his human dignity. In this manner were 'confessions' acquired.

When the wave of mass arrests began to recede in 1939, and the leaders of territorial party organizations began to accuse the NKVD workers of using methods of physical pressure on the arrested, Stalin dispatched a coded telegram on January 20, 1939 to the committee secretaries of oblasts and krais, to the central committees of republic communist parties, to the people's commissars for internal affairs and to the heads of NKVD organizations. This telegram stated:

> The Central Committee of the All-Union Communist Party (Bolsheviks) explains that the application of methods of physical pressure in NKVD practice has been permissible from 1937 on in accordance with permission of the Central Committee of the All-Union Communist Party (Bolsheviks). . . . It is known that all bourgeois intelligence services use methods of physical coercion against the representatives of the socialist proletariat and that they use them in their most scandalous form. The question arises as to why the socialist intelligence service should be more humanitarian against the mad agents of the bourgeoisie, against the deadly enemies of the working class and the kolkhoz workers. The Central Committee of the All-Union Communist Party (Bolsheviks) considers that physical pressure should still be used obligatorily, as an exception applicable to known and obstinate enemies of the people, as a method both justifiable and appropriate.

Thus, Stalin sanctioned in the name of the Central Committee of the All-Union Communist Party (Bolsheviks) the most brutal violation of socialist legality, torture and oppression, which led as we have seen to the slandering and self-accusation of innocent people.

Not long ago — only a few days before the present congress — we called to the Central Committee Presidium session and interrogated the investigating judge Rodos, who in his time investigated and interrogated Kosior, Chubar[18] and Kosarev.[19] He is a vile person, with the brain of a bird, and morally completely degenerate. And it was this man who decided the fate of prominent party workers; he also made judgments on the politics of these matters, because having established their 'crime', he provided therewith materials from which important political implications could be drawn.

The question arises whether a man with such an intellect could alone make the investigation in a manner to prove the guilt of people such as Kosior and others. No, he could not have done it without proper directives. At the Central Committee Presidium session he told us: 'I was told that Kosior and Chubar were enemies of the people and for this reason, I, as investigating judge, had to make them confess that they were enemies'. (*Indignation in the hall.*)

He could do this only through long tortures, which he did, receiving detailed instructions from Beria.[20] We must say that at the Central Committee Presidium session he cynically declared: 'I thought that I was executing the orders of the party'. In this manner Stalin's orders concerning the use of methods of physical pressure against the arrested were in practice executed.

These and many other facts show that all norms of correct party solution of problems were invalidated and everything was dependent upon the willfulness of one man.

The power accumulated in the hands of one person, Stalin, led to serious consequences during the Great Patriotic War.

When we look at many of our novels, films and historical 'scientific studies', the role of Stalin in the Patriotic War appears to be entirely improbable. Stalin had foreseen everything. The Soviet Army, on the basis of a strategic plan prepared by Stalin long before, used the tactics of so-called 'active defense', i.e., tactics which, as we know, allowed the Germans to come up to Moscow and Stalingrad. Using such tactics the Soviet Army, supposedly thanks only to Stalin's genius, turned to the offensive and subdued the enemy. The epic victory gained through the armed might of the Land of the Soviets, through our heroic people is ascribed in this type of novel, film and 'scientific study' as being completely due to the strategic genius of Stalin.

We have to analyze this matter carefully because it has a tremendous significance not only from the historical, but especially from the political, educational and practical point of view.

What are the facts of this matter?

Before the war our press and all our political-educational work was characterized by its bragging tone: when an enemy violates the holy Soviet soil, then for every blow of the enemy we will answer with three blows and we will battle the enemy on his soil and we will win without much harm to ourselves. But these positive statements were not based in all areas on concrete facts, which would actually guarantee the immunity of our borders.

During the war and after the war Stalin put forward the thesis that the tragedy which our nation experienced in the first part of the war was the result of the 'unexpected' attack of the Germans against the Soviet Union. But, Comrades, this is completely untrue. As soon as Hitler came to power in Germany he assigned himself the task of liquidating communism. The fascists were saying this openly; they did not hide their plans. In order to attain this aggressive end all sorts of pacts and blocs were created, such as the famous Berlin-Rome-Tokyo axis. Many facts from the pre-war period clearly showed that Hitler was going all out to begin a war against the Soviet state and that he had concentrated large armed units, together with armored units, near the Soviet borders.

Documents which have now been published show that by April 3, 1941, Churchill, through his ambassador to the U.S.S.R., Cripps, personally warned Stalin that the Germans had begun regrouping their armed units with the intent of attacking the Soviet Union. It is self-evident that Churchill did not do this at all because of his friendly feeling toward the Soviet nation. He had in this his own imperialistic goals — to bring Germany and the U.S.S.R. into a bloody war and thereby to strengthen the position of the British Empire. Just the same, Churchill affirmed in his writings that he sought to 'warn Stalin and call his attention to the danger which threatened him'. Churchill stressed this repeatedly in his dispatches of April 18 and in the following days. However, Stalin took no heed of these warnings. What is more, Stalin ordered that no credence be given to information of this sort, in order not to provoke the initiation of military operations.

We must assert that information of this sort concerning the threat of German armed invasion of Soviet territory was coming in also from our own military and diplomatic sources; however, because the leadership was conditioned against such information, such data was dispatched with fear and assessed with reservation.

Thus, for instance, information sent from Berlin on May 6, 1941, by the Soviet military attaché, Capt. Vorontsov, stated:

> Soviet citizen Bozer . . . communicated to the deputy naval attaché that according to a statement of a certain German officer from Hitler's Headquarters, Germany is preparing to invade the USSR on May 14 through Finland, the Baltic countries and Latvia. At the same time Moscow and Leningrad will be heavily raided and paratroopers landed in border cities. . . .

In his report of May 22, 1941, the deputy military attaché in Berlin, Khlopov, communicated that ' . . . the attack of the

German army is reportedly scheduled for June 15, but it is possible that it may begin in the first days of June. . . . '

A cable from our London Embassy dated June 18, 1941 stated:

> As of now Cripps is deeply convinced of the inevitability of armed conflict between Germany and the USSR which will begin not later than the middle of June. According to Cripps, the Germans have presently concentrated 147 divisions (including air force and service units) along the Soviet borders. . . .

Despite these particularly grave warnings, the necessary steps were not taken to prepare the country properly for defense and to prevent it from being caught unawares.

Did we have time and the capabilities for such preparations? Yes, we had the time and capabilities. Our industry was already so developed that it was capable of fully supplying the Soviet army with everything that it needed. This is proven by the fact that although during the war we lost almost half of our industry and important industrial and food production areas as the result of enemy occupation of the Ukraine, Northern Caucasus and other western parts of the country, the Soviet people was still able to organize the production of military equipment in the eastern parts of the country, install there equipment taken from the western industrial areas, and to supply our armed forces with everything which was necessary to destroy the enemy.

Had our industry been mobilized properly and in time to supply the army with the necessary *matériel,* our war-time losses would have been decidedly smaller. Such mobilization had not been, however, started in time. And already in the first days of the war it became evident that our army was badly armed, that we did not have enough artillery, tanks and planes to throw the enemy back.

Soviet science and technology produced excellent models of tanks and artillery pieces before the war. But mass production of all this was not organized and as a matter of fact we started to modernize our military equipment only on the eve of the war. As a result, at the time of the enemy's invasion of the Soviet land we did not have sufficient quantities either of old machinery which was no longer used for armament production or of new machinery which we had planned to introduce into armament production. The situation with anti-aircraft artillery was especially bad; we did not organize the production of anti-tank ammunition. Many fortified regions had proven to be indefensible as soon as they were attacked, because the old arms had been withdrawn and new ones were not yet available there.

This pertained, alas, not only to tanks, artillery and planes. At the outbreak of the war we did not even have sufficient numbers of rifles to arm the mobilized manpower. I recall that in those days I telephoned to Comrade Malenkov from Kiev and told him, 'People have volunteered for the new army and demand arms. You must send us arms'.

Malenkov answered me, 'We cannot send you arms. We are sending all our rifles to Leningrad and you have to arm yourselves'. (*Movement in the hall.*)

Such was the armament situation.

In this connection we cannot forget, for instance, the following fact. Shortly before the invasion of the Soviet Union by the Hitlerite army, Kirponos, who was Chief of the Kiev Special Military District (he was later killed at the front), wrote to Stalin that the German armies were at the Bug River, were preparing for an attack and in the very near future would probably start their offensive. In this connection Kirponos proposed that a strong defense be organized, that 300,000 people be evacuated from the border areas and that several strong points be organized there: anti-tank ditches, trenches for the soldiers, etc.

Moscow answered this proposition with the assertion that this would be a provocation, that no preparatory defensive work should be undertaken at the borders, that the Germans were not to be given any pretext for the initiation of military action against us. Thus, our borders were insufficiently prepared to repel the enemy.

When the fascist armies had actually invaded Soviet territory and military operations began, Moscow issued the order that the German fire was not to be returned. Why? It was because Stalin, despite evident facts, thought that the war had not yet started, that this was only a provocative action on the part of several undisciplined sections of the German army, and that our reaction might serve as a pretext for the Germans to begin the war.

The following fact is also known. On the eve of the invasion of the territory of the Soviet Union by the Hitlerite army a certain German citizen crossed our border and stated that the German armies had received orders to start the offensive against the Soviet Union on the night of June 22, at 3 o'clock. Stalin was informed about this immediately, but even this warning was ignored.

As you see, everything was ignored: warnings of certain army commanders, declarations of deserters from the enemy army, and even the open hostility of the enemy. Is this an example of the alertness of the chief of the party and the state at this particularly significant historical moment?

And what were the results of this carefree attitude, this disregard of clear facts? The result was that already in the first hours and days the enemy destroyed in our border regions a large part of our air force, artillery and other military equipment; he annihilated large numbers of our military cadres and disorganized our military leadership; consequently we could not prevent the enemy from marching deep into the country.

Very grievous consequences, especially in reference to the beginning of the war, followed from Stalin's annihilation of many military commanders and political workers during 1937-1941 because of his suspiciousness and through slanderous accusations.[21] During these years repressions were instituted against certain parts of military cadres beginning literally at the company and battalion commander level and extending to the higher military centers; during this time the cadre of leaders who had gained military experience in Spain and in the Far East was almost completely liquidated.

The policy of large-scale repression against the military cadres led also to undermined military discipline, because for several years officers of all ranks and even soldiers in the party and komsomol cells were taught to 'unmask' their superiors as hidden enemies. (*Movement in the hall.*) It is natural that this produced a negative effect on the state of military discipline in the first war period.

And, as you know, we had before the war excellent military cadres which were unquestionably loyal to the party and to the fatherland. Suffice it to say that those of them who managed to survive despite severe tortures to which they were subjected in the prisons, showed themselves from the first days of the war to be real patriots and heroically fought for the glory of the fatherland; I have here in mind such comrades as Rokossovsky (who, as you know, had been jailed), Gorbatov, Meretskov (who is a delegate at the present congress), Podlas (he was an excellent commander who perished at the front), and many, many others. However, many such commanders perished in camps and jails and the army saw them no more.

All this brought about the situation which existed at the beginning of the war and which was a great threat to our fatherland.

It would be wrong to forget that after the first severe disaster and defeats at the front, Stalin thought that this was the end. In one of his speeches in those days he said: 'All that Lenin created we have lost forever'.

After this Stalin for a long time actually did not direct the military operations and ceased to do anything whatever. He returned to active leadership only when some members of the Political Bureau visited him and told him that it was necessary to take certain steps immediately in order to improve the situation at the front.

Therefore, the threatening danger which hung over our fatherland in the first period of the war was largely due to the faulty methods of directing the nation and the party by Stalin himself.

However, we speak not only about the moment when the war began, which led to serious disorganization of our army and brought us severe losses. Even after the war began, the nervousness and hysteria which Stalin demonstrated, interfering with actual military operations, caused our army serious damage.

Stalin was very far from an understanding of the real situation which was developing at the front. This was natural because during the whole Patriotic War he never visited any section of the front or any liberated city except for one short ride on the Mozhaisk Highway during a stabilized situation at the front. To this incident were dedicated many literary works full of fantasies of all sorts and so many paintings. Simultaneously, Stalin was interfering with operations and issuing orders which did not take into consideration the real situation at a given section of the front and which could not help but result in huge personnel losses.

I will allow myself in this connection to bring out one characteristic fact which illustrates how Stalin directed operations at the fronts. There is present at this Congress Marshal Bagramyan who was once the Chief of Operations in the Headquarters of the Southwestern Front and who can corroborate what I will tell you.

When there developed an exceptionally serious situation for our army in 1942 in the Kharkov region, we correctly decided to drop an operation whose objective had been to encircle Kharkov, because the real situation at that time would have threatened our army with fatal consequences if this operation had been proceeded with.

We communicated this to Stalin, stating that the situation demanded changes in operational plans in order to prevent the enemy from liquidating a sizable concentration of our army.

Contrary to common sense, Stalin rejected our suggestion and issued the order to continue the operation aimed at the encirclement of Kharkov, despite the fact that at this time many army concentrations were themselves actually threatened with encirclement and liquidation.

I telephoned Vasilevsky and begged him, 'Alexander Mikhailovich, take a map (Vasilevsky is present here) and show Comrade Stalin the situation which has developed.' We should note that Stalin planned operations on a globe. (*Animation in the hall.*) Yes, comrades, he used to take the globe and trace the frontline on it. I said to Comrade Vasilevsky: 'Show him the situation on a map; in the present situation we cannot continue the operation which was planned. The old decision must be changed for the good of the cause'.

Vasilevsky replied saying that Stalin had already studied this problem and that he, Vasilevsky, would not see Stalin further concerning this matter, because the latter didn't want to hear any arguments on the subject of this operation.

After my talk with Vasilevsky I telephone Stalin at his villa. But Stalin did not answer the telephone and Malenkov was at the receiver. I told Comrade Malenkov that I was calling from the front and that I wanted to speak personally to Stalin. Stalin informed me through Malenkov that I should speak with Malenkov. I stated for the second time that I wished to inform Stalin personally about the grave situation which had arisen for us at the front. But Stalin did not consider it convenient to pick up the phone and again stated that I should speak to him through Malenkov, although he was only a few steps from the telephone.

After 'listening' in this manner to our plea Stalin said, 'Let everything remain as it is!'

And what was the result of this? The worst that we had expected. The Germans surrounded our army concentrations and consequently we lost hundreds of thousands of our soldiers. This is Stalin's military 'genius'; this what it cost us. (*Movement in the hall.*)

On one occasion after the war, during a meeting of Stalin with members of the Political Bureau, Anastas Ivanovich Mikoyan mentioned that Khrushchev must have been right when he telephoned concerning the Kharkov operation and that it was unfortunate that his suggestion had not been accepted.

You should have seen Stalin's fury! How could it be admitted that he, Stalin, had not been right. He is after all a 'genius', and a genius cannot help but be right! Everyone can err, but Stalin considered that he never erred, that he was always right. He never acknowledged to anyone that he had made any mistake, large or small, despite the fact that he made not a few mistakes in the matter of theory and in his practical activity. After the party congress we shall probably have to re-evaluate many wartime military operations and to present them in their true light.

The tactics on which Stalin insisted without knowing the essence of the conduct of battle operations cost us much blood until we succeeded in stopping our adversaries and going over to the offensive.

The military know that already by the end of 1941 instead of great operational manoeuvres flanking our adversaries and penetrating to their rear, Stalin demanded incessant frontal attacks and the capture of one village after another. Because of this we paid with great losses until our generals, on whose shoulders rested the whole weight of conducting the war, succeeded in changing the situation and shifting to flexible manoeuvre operations, which immediately brought serious changes at the front favorable to us.

All the more shameful was the fact that after our great victory over the enemy which cost us so much, Stalin began to downgrade many of the commanders who contributed so much to the victory over the enemy, because Stalin excluded every possibility that services rendered at the front should be credited to anyone but himself.

Stalin was very much interested in the assessment of Comrade Zhukov as a military leader. He asked me often for my opinion of Zhukov. I told him then, 'I have known Zhukov for a long time; he is a good general and a good military leader'.

After the war Stalin began to tell all kinds of nonsense about Zhukov, among others the following,

> You praised Zhukov, but he does not deserve it. It is said that before each operation at the front Zhukov used to behave as follows: he used to take a handful of earth, smell it and say, 'We can begin the attack', or the opposite, 'The planned operation cannot be carried out'.

I stated at that time, 'Comrade Stalin, I do not know who invented this, but it is not true'. It is possible that Stalin himself invented these things for the purpose of minimizing the role and military talents of Marshal Zhukov.[22]

In this connection Stalin very energetically popularized himself as a great leader; in various ways he tried to inculcate in the people the version that all victories gained by the Soviet nation during the Great Patriotic War were due to the courage, daring and genius of Stalin and to no one else. Exactly like Kuzma Kryuchkov[23] he put one dress on 7 people at the same time. (*Animation in the hall.*)

In the same vein, let us take, for instance, our historical and military films and some works of literature; they make us feel sick. Their true objective is the propagation of the theme of praising Stalin as a military genius. Let us recall the film, 'The Fall of Berlin'. Here only Stalin acts; he issues orders in the hall in which there are many empty chairs and only one man approaches him and reports something to him — that is Poskrebyshev,[24] his loyal shieldbearer. (*Laughter in the hall.*)

And where is the military command? Where is the Political Bureau? Where is the Government? What are they doing and with what are they engaged? There is nothing about them in the film. Stalin acts for everybody; he does not reckon with anyone, he asks no one for advice. Everything is shown to the nation in this false light. Why? In order to surround Stalin with glory, contrary to the facts and contrary to historical truth.

The question arises: And where are the military on whose shoulders rested the burden of the war? They are not in the film, with Stalin in, no room was left for them.

Not Stalin, but the party as a whole, the Soviet Government, our heroic army, its talented leaders and brave soldiers, the whole Soviet nation — these are the ones who assured the victory in the Great Patriotic War. (*Tempestuous and prolonged applause.*)

The Central Committee members, ministers, our economic leaders, leaders of Soviet culture, directors of territorial party and soviet organizations, engineers, and technicians — every one of them in his own place of work generously gave of his strength and knowledge toward ensuring victory over the enemy.

Exceptional heroism was shown by our hard core — surrounded by glory is our whole working class, our kolkhoz peasantry, the Soviet intelligentsia, who under the leadership of party organizations overcame untold hardships and, bearing the hardships of war, devoted all their strength to the cause of the defense of the fatherland.

Great and brave deeds during the war were accomplished by our Soviet women who bore on their backs the heavy load of production work in the factories, on the kolkhozes, and in various economic and cultural sectors; many women participated directly in the Great Patriotic War at the fronts; our brave youth contributed immeasurably at the front and at home to the defense of the Soviet fatherland and to the annihilation of the enemy.

Immortal are the services of the Soviet soldiers, of our commanders and political workers of all ranks; after the loss of a considerable part of the army in the first months of the war they did not lose their heads and were able to reorganize during the progress of combat; they created and toughened during the progress of the war a strong and heroic army and not only withstood the pressure of a strong and cunning enemy but also smashed him.

The magnificent and heroic deeds of hundreds of millions of people of the East and of the West during the fight against the threat of fascist subjugation which loomed before us will live for centuries and millenia in the memory of a thankful humanity. (*Thunderous applause.*)

The main role and the main credit for the victorious ending of the war belongs to our communist party, to the armed forces of the Soviet Union, and to the tens of millions of Soviet people raised by the party. (*Thunderous and prolonged applause.*)

Comrades, let us reach for some other facts. The Soviet Union is justly considered as a model of a multi-national state because we have in practice assured the equality and friendship of all nations which live in our great fatherland.

All the more monstrous are the acts whose initiator was Stalin and which represent crude violations of the basic Leninist principles of the nationality policy of the Soviet state. We refer to the mass deportations from their native places of whole nations, together with all communists and komsomol members without any exception; this deportation action was not dictated by any military considerations.

Thus, as early as the end of 1943, when there occurred a permanent breakthrough at the fronts of the Great Patriotic War benefiting the Soviet Union, a decision was taken and carried out concerning the deportation of all the Karachai from the lands on which they lived. In the same period, at the end of December 1943, the same lot befell the whole population of the Kalmyk Autonomous Republic. In March 1944 all the Chechen and Ingush peoples were deported and the Chechen-Ingush Autonomous Republic was liquidated. In April 1944, all Balkars were deported to faraway places from the territory of the Kabardino-Balkar Autonomous Republic and the Republic itself was renamed the Karbardin Autonomous Republic.[25] The Ukrainians avoided meeting this fate only because there were too many of them and there was no place to which to deport them. Otherwise, he would have deported them also. (*Laughter and animation in the hall.*)

Not only no Marxist-Leninist but no man of common sense can grasp how it is possible to make whole nations responsible for hostile activity, including women, children, old people, communists and komsomol members, to use mass repression against them, and to expose them to misery and suffering for the hostile acts of individual persons or groups of persons.

After the conclusion of the Patriotic War the Soviet nation stressed with pride the magnificent victories gained through great sacrifices and tremendous efforts. The country experienced a period of political enthusiasm. The party came out of the war even more united; in the fire of the war party cadres were tempered and hardened. Under such conditions nobody could have even thought of the possibility of some plot in the party.

And it was precisely at this time that the so-called 'Leningrad affair' was born. As we have now proven, this case was fabricated. Those who innocently lost their lives included Comrades Voznesensky, Kuznetsov, Rodionov, Popkov, and others.[26]

As is known, Voznesensky and Kuznetsov were talented and eminent leaders. Once they stood very close to Stalin. It is sufficient to mention that Stalin made Voznesensky a First Deputy

Chairman of the Council of Ministers and Kuznetsov was elected a Secretary of the Central Committee. The very fact that Stalin entrusted Kuznetsov with the supervision of the state security organs shows the trust which he enjoyed.

How did it happen that these persons were branded as enemies of the people and liquidated?

Facts prove that the 'Leningrad affair' is also the result of willfulness which Stalin exercised against party cadres.

Had a normal situation existed in the party's Central Committee and in the Central Committee Political Bureau, affairs of this nature would have been examined there in accordance with party practice, and all pertinent facts assessed; as a result such an affair as well as others would not have happened.

We must state that after the war the situation became even more complicated. Stalin became even more capricious, irritable and brutal; in particular his suspicion grew. His persecution mania reached unbelievable dimensions. Many workers were becoming enemies before his very eyes. After the war Stalin separated himself from the collective even more. Everything was decided by him alone without any consideration for anyone or anything.

This unbelievable suspicion was cleverly taken advantage of by the abject provocateur and vile enemy, Beria, who murdered thousands of communists and loyal Soviet people. The elevation of Voznesensky and Kuznetsov alarmed Beria. As we have now proven, it was precisely Beria who 'suggested' to Stalin the fabrication by him and by his confidants of materials in the form of declarations and anonymous letters, and in the form of various rumors and talks.

The party's Central Committee has examined this so-called 'Leningrad affair'; the persons who innocently suffered are now rehabilitated and honor has been restored to the glorious Leningrad party organization. Abakumov[27] and others who fabricated this affair have been brought before a court; their trial took place in Leningrad and they received what they deserved.

The question arises: Why is it that we see the truth of this affair only now, and why did we not do something earlier, during Stalin's life, in order to prevent the loss of innocent lives? It was because Stalin supervised the 'Leningrad affair' personally and the majority of the Political Bureau members did not, at that time, know all of the circumstances in these matters, and could not therefore intervene.

When Stalin received certain materials from Beria and Abakumov, without examining these slanderous materials, he ordered an investigation of the 'affair' of Voznesensky and Kuznetsov. With this their fate was sealed. Instructive in the same way is the case of the Mingrelian nationalist organization which allegedly existed in Georgia.[28] As is known, resolutions by the Central Committee [of the] Communist Party of the Soviet Union were made concerning this case in November 1951 and in March 1952.[29] These resolutions were made without prior discussion with the Political Bureau. Stalin personally dictated them. They made serious accusations against many loyal communists. On the basis of falsified documents it was proven that there existed in Georgia an allegedly nationalistic organization whose objective was the liquidation of Soviet power in that republic with the help of imperialist powers.

In this connection, a number of responsible party and soviet workers were arrested in Georgia. As was later proven, this was a slander directed against the Georgian party organization.

We know that there have been at times manifestations of local bourgeois nationalism in Georgia as in several other republics. The question arises: Could it be possible that in the period when the resolutions referred to above were made, nationalist tendencies had grown to such a point that there was a danger of Georgia's leaving the Soviet Union and joining Turkey? (*Animation in the hall, laughter.*)

This is, of course, nonsense. It is impossible to imagine how such assumptions could enter anyone's mind. Everyone knows how Georgia has developed economically and culturally under Soviet rule.

Industrial production in the Georgian Republic is 27 times greater than it was before the revolution. Many new industries have arisen in Georgia which did not exist there before the revolution: iron smelting, an oil industry, a machine construction industry, etc. Illiteracy, which, in pre-revolutionary Georgia, included 78 percent of the population, has long since been liquidated.

Could the Georgians, comparing the situation in their republic with the hard situation of the working masses in Turkey, be aspiring to join Turkey? In 1955 Georgia produced 18 times as much steel per person as Turkey. Georgia produces 9 times as much electrical energy per person as Turkey. According to the available 1950 census, 65 percent of Turkey's total population are illiterate, and of the women, 80 percent are illiterate. Georgia has 19 institutions of higher learning which have about 39,000 students; this is 8 times more than in Turkey (for each 1,000 inhabitants). The prosperity of the working people has grown tremendously in Georgia under Soviet rule.

It is clear that as the economy and culture develop, and as the socialist consciousness of the working masses in Georgia grows, the source from which bourgeois nationalism draws its strength evaporates.

As it turned out, there was no nationalistic organization in Georgia. Thousands of innocent people fell victims to willfulness and lawlessness. All of this happened under the 'genius' leadership of Stalin, 'the great son of the Georgian nation', as Georgians liked to refer to Stalin. (*Animation in the hall.*)

The willfulness of Stalin showed itself not only in decisions concerning the internal life of the country but also in the international relations of the Soviet Union.

The July plenary session of the Central Committee studied in detail the reasons for the development of conflict with Yugoslavia. It was a shameful role which Stalin played here. The 'Yugoslav affair' contained no problems which could not have been solved through party discussions among comrades. There was no significant basis for the development of this 'affair'; it was completely possible to have prevented the rupture of relations with that country. This does not mean, however, that the Yugoslav leaders did not make mistakes or did not have shortcomings. But these mistakes and shortcomings were magnified in a monstrous manner by Stalin, which resulted in a break of relations with a friendly country.

I recall the first days when the conflict between the Soviet Union and Yugoslavia began artificially to be blown up. Once, when I came from Kiev to Moscow, I was invited to visit Stalin who, pointing to the copy of a letter lately sent to Tito, asked me, 'Have you read this?' Not waiting for my reply he answered, 'I will shake my little finger — and there will be no more Tito. He will fall'.

We have paid dearly for this 'shaking of the little finger'. This statement reflected Stalin's mania for greatness, but that is just the way he acted: 'I will shake my little finger — and there will be no Kosior'; 'I will shake my little finger once more and Postyshev and Chubar will be no more'; 'I will shake my little finger again — and Voznesensky, Kuznetsov and many others will disappear'.

But this did not happen to Tito. No matter how much or how little Stalin shook, not only his little finger but everything else that he could shake, Tito did not fall. Why? The reason was that, in this case of disagreement with the Yugoslav comrades, Tito had behind him a state and a people who had gone through a severe school of fighting for liberty and independence, a people which gave support to its leaders.

You see to what Stalin's mania for greatness led. He lost all awareness of reality; he demonstrated his suspicion and haughtiness not only in relation to individuals in the U.S.S.R., but in relation to whole parties and nations.

We have carefully examined the case of Yugoslavia and have found a proper solution which is approved by the peoples of the Soviet Union and of Yugoslavia as well as by the working masses of all the people's democracies and by all progressive humanity. The liquidation of the abnormal relationship with Yugoslavia was done in the interests of the whole camp of socialism, in the interests of strengthening peace in the whole world.

Let us also recall the 'affair of the doctor-plotters'. (*Animation in the hall.*) Actually there was no 'affair' apart from a declaration by the woman doctor Timashuk, who was probably influenced or ordered by someone (after all, she was an unofficial collaborator of the organs of state security) to write Stalin a letter in which she declared that doctors were applying allegedly improper methods of medical treatment.

Such a letter was sufficient for Stalin to reach an immediate conclusion that there were doctor-plotters in the Soviet Union. He issued orders to arrest a group of eminent Soviet medical specialists. He personally issued advice on the conduct of the investigation and the method of interrogation of the arrested persons. He said that academician Vinogradov should be put in chains, another one should be beaten. Present at this congress as a delegate is the former Minister for State Security, Comrade Ignatiev. Stalin told him curtly, 'If you do not obtain confessions from the doctors we will shorten you by a head'. (*Tumult in the hall.*)

Stalin personally called the investigating judge, gave him instructions, and advised him on what investigating methods should be used; these methods were simple — beat, beat and, once again, beat.

Shortly after the doctors were arrested we members of the Political Bureau received protocols with the doctors' confessions of guilt. After distributing these protocols Stalin told us, 'You are blind like young kittens; what will happen without me? The country will perish because you do not know how to recognize enemies'.

The case was so presented that no one could verify the facts on which the investigation was based. There was no possibility of trying to verify facts by contacting those who had made the confessions of guilt.

We felt, however, that the case of the arrested doctors was questionable. We knew some of these people personally because they had once treated us. When we examined this 'case' after Stalin's death, we found it to be fabricated from beginning to end.

This ignominious 'case' was set up by Stalin; he did not, however, have the time in which to bring it to an end (as he conceived that end), and for this reason the doctors are still alive. Now all have been rehabilitated; they are working in the same places they were working before; they treat top individuals, not excluding members of the government; they have our full confidence; and they execute their duties honestly, as they did before.

In organizing the various dirty and shameful cases, a very base role was played by the rabid enemy of our party, the foreign intelligence agent Beria, who had stolen into Stalin's confidence.[30] In what way could this provocateur gain such a position in the party and in the state, so as to become First Deputy Chairman of the Council of Ministers of the Soviet Union and a member of the Central Committee Political Bureau? It has now been established that this villain climbed up the government ladder over an untold number of corpses.

Were there any signs that Beria was an enemy of the party? Yes, there were. Already in 1937, at a plenary session of the Central Committee, the former People's Commissar for Health Kaminsky said that Beria worked for the Mussavat intelligence service.[31] But the plenary session of the Central Committee had barely concluded when Kaminsky was arrested and then shot. Had Stalin examined Kaminsky's statement? No, because Stalin believed in Beria, and that was enough for him. And when

Stalin believed in anyone or anything, then no one could say anything which was contrary to his opinion; anyone who would dare to express opposition would have met the same fate as Kaminsky.

There were other signs also. The declaration which Comrade Snegov made to the Party's Central Committee is interesting. (Parenthetically speaking, he was also rehabilitated not long ago, after 17 years in prison camps.) In this declaration Snegov writes:

> In connection with the proposed rehabilitation of the former Central Committee member, Kartvelishvili-Lavrentiev, I have entrusted to the hands of the representative of the Committee of State Security a detailed deposition concerning Beria's role in the disposition of the Kartvelishvili case and concerning the criminal motives by which Beria was guided.
>
> In my opinion it is indispensable to recall an important fact pertaining to this case and to communicate it to the Central Committee, because I did not consider it as proper to include it in the investigation documents.
>
> On October 30, 1931, at the session of the Organizational Bureau of the Central Committee, All-Union Communist Party (Bolsheviks), Kartvelishvili, Secretary of the Transcaucasian Krai Committee, made a report. All members of the Executive of the Krai Committee were present; of them I alone am alive. During this session J. V. Stalin proposed a motion at the end of his speech concerning the organization of the Secretariat of the Transcaucasian Krai Committee composed of the following: First Secretary, Kartvelishvili; Second Secretary, Beria (it was then for the first time in the party's history that Beria's name was mentioned as a candidate for a party position). Kartvelishvili answered that he knew Beria well and for that reason refused categorically to work together with him. Stalin proposed then that this matter be left open and that it be solved in the process of the work itself. Two days later a decision was arrived at that Beria would receive the party post and that Kartvelishvili would be deported from the Transcaucasus.

This fact can be confirmed by Comrades Mikoyan and Kaganovich who were present at that session.

The long unfriendly relations between Kartvelishvili and Beria were widely known; they date back to the time when Comrade Sergo[32] was active in the Transcaucasus; Kartvelishvili was Sergo's closest assistant. The unfriendly relationship impelled Beria to fabricate a 'case' against Kartvelishvili.

It is a characteristic thing that in this 'case' Kartvelishvili was charged with a terroristic act against Beria.

The indictment in the Beria case contains a discussion of his crimes. Some things should, however, be recalled, especially since it is possible that not all delegates to the congress have read this document. I wish to recall Beria's bestial disposition of the cases of Kedrov, Golubiev, and Golubiev's adopted mother, Baturina — persons who wished to inform the Central Committee concerning Beria's treacherous activity. They were shot without any trial and the sentence was passed ex-post facto, after the execution.

Here is what the old communist, Comrade Kedrov,[33] wrote to the Central Committee through Comrade Andreev (Comrade Andreev was then a Central Committee secretary):

> I am calling to you for help from a gloomy cell of the Lefortovo prison. Let my cry of horror reach your ears; do not remain deaf; take me under your protection; please, help remove the nightmare of interrogations and show that this is all a mistake.
>
> I suffer innocently. Please believe me. Time will testify to the truth. I am not an agent-provocateur of the Tsarist Okhrana; I am not a spy; I am not a member of an anti-Soviet organization of which I am being accused on the basis of denunciations. I am also not guilty of any other crimes against the party and the government. I am an old bolshevik, free of any stain; I have honestly fought for almost 40 years in the ranks of the party for the good and the prosperity of the nation. . . .
>
> . . . Today I, a 62-year-old man, am being threatened by the investigating judges with more severe, cruel and degrading methods of physical pressure. They [the judges] are no longer capable of becoming aware of their error and of recognizing that their handling of my case is illegal and impermissible. They try to justify their actions by picturing me as a hardened and raving enemy and are demanding increased repressions. But let the party know that I am

innocent and that there is nothing which can turn a loyal son of the party into an enemy, even right up to his last dying breath.

But I have no way out. I cannot divert from myself the hastily approaching new and powerful blows.

Everything, however, has its limits. My torture has reached the extreme. My health is broken, my strength and my energy are waning, the end is drawing near. To die in a Soviet prison, branded as a vile traitor to the fatherland — what can be more monstrous for an honest man. And how monstrous all this is! Unsurpassed bitterness and pain grips my heart. No! No! This will not happen; this cannot be — I cry. Neither the party, nor the Soviet government, nor the People's Commissar, L. P. Beria, will permit this cruel irreparable injustice. I am firmly certain that given a quiet, objective examination, without any foul rantings, without any anger and without the fearful tortures, it would be easy to prove the baselessness of the charges. I believe deeply that truth and justice will triumph. I believe. I believe.

The old Bolshevik, Comrade Kedrov, was found innocent by the Military Collegium. But despite this, he was shot at Beria's order. (*Indignation in the hall.*)

Beria also handled cruelly the family of Comrade Ordzhonikidze. Why? Because Ordzhonikidze had tried to prevent Beria from realizing his shameful plans. Beria cleared from his way all persons who could possibly interfere with him. Ordzonikidze was always an opponent of Beria, which he told to Stalin. Instead of examining this affair and taking appropriate steps, Stalin allowed the liquidation of Ordzhonikidze's brother and brought Ordzhonikidze himself to such a state that he was forced to shoot himself.[34] (*Indignation in the hall.*) Such was Beria.

Beria was unmasked by the Party's Central Committee shortly after Stalin's death. As a result of particularly detailed legal proceedings it was established that Beria had committed monstrous crimes and Beria was shot.

The question arises why Beria, who had liquidated tens of thousands of party and soviet workers, was not unmasked during Stalin's life? He was not unmasked earlier because he utilized very skillfully Stalin's weaknesses; feeding him with suspicions, he assisted Stalin in everything and acted with his support.

Comrades! The cult of the individual acquired such monstrous size chiefly because Stalin himself, using all conceivable methods, supported the glorification of his own person. This is supported by numerous facts. One of the most characteristic examples of Stalin's self-glorification and of his lack of even elementary modesty is the edition of his *Short Biography,* which was published in 1948.

This book is an expression of the most dissolute flattery, an example of making a man into a godhead, of transforming him into an infallible sage, 'the greatest leader', 'sublime strategist of all times and nations'. Finally no other words could be found with which to lift Stalin up to the heavens.

We need not give here examples of the loathsome adulation filling this book. All we need to add is that they were all approved and edited by Stalin personally and some of them were added in his own handwriting to the draft text of the book.

What did Stalin consider essential to write into this book? Did he want to cool the ardor of his flatterers who were composing his *Short Biography*? No! He marked the very places where he thought that the praise of his services was insufficient.

Here are some examples characterizing Stalin's activity, added in Stalin's own hand:

> In this fight against the skeptics and capitulators, the Trotskyites, Zinovievites, Bukharinites and Kamenevites, there was definitely welded together, after Lenin's death, that leading core of the party[35] . . . that upheld the great banner of Lenin, rallied the party behind Lenin's behests, and brought the Soviet people into the broad road of industrializing the country and collectivising the rural economy. The leader of this core and the guiding force of the party and the state was Comrade Stalin.

Thus writes Stalin himself! Then he adds:

> Although he performed his task of leader of the party and the people with consummate skill and enjoyed the unreserved support of the entire Soviet people, Stalin never allowed his work to be marred by the slightest hint of vanity, conceit or self-adulation.

Where and when could a leader so praise himself? Is this worthy of a leader of the Marxist-Leninist type? No. Precisely

71

against this did Marx and Engels take such a strong position. This also was always sharply condemned by Vladimir Ilyich Lenin.

In the draft text of his book appeared the following sentence: 'Stalin is the Lenin of today'. This sentence appeared to Stalin to be too weak, so in his own handwriting he changed it to read: 'Stalin is the worthy continuer of Lenin's work, or, as it is said in our party, Stalin is the Lenin of today'. You see how well it is said, not by the nation but by Stalin himself.

It is possible to give many such self-praising appraisals written into the draft text of that book in Stalin's hand. Especially generously does he endow himself with praises pertaining to his military genius, to his talent for strategy.

I will cite one more insertion made by Stalin on the theme of Stalin's military genius.

'The advanced Soviet science of war received further development', he writes,

> at Comrade Stalin's hands. Comrade Stalin elaborated the theory of the permanently operating factors that decide the issue of wars, of active defense and the laws of counter-offensive and offensive, of the co-operation of all services and arms in modern warfare, of the role of big tank masses and air forces in modern war, and of the artillery as the most formidable of the armed services. At the various stages of the war Stalin's genius found the correct solutions that took account of all the circumstances of the situation. (*Movement in the hall.*)

And further, writes Stalin:

> Stalin's military mastership was displayed both in defense and offense. Comrade Stalin's genius enabled him to divine the enemy's plans and defeat them. The battles in which Comrade Stalin directed the Soviet armies are brilliant examples of operational military skill.

In this manner was Stalin praised as a strategist. Who did this? Stalin himself, not in his role as strategist but in the role of author-editor, one of the main creators of his self-adulatory biography.

Such, comrades, are the facts. We should rather say the shameful facts.

And one additional fact from the same *Short Biography* of Stalin. As is known, *The Short Course of the History of the All-Union Communist Party (Bolsheviks)* was written by a commission of the Party's Central Committee.

This book, parenthetically, was also permeated with the cult of the individual and was written by a designated group of authors. This fact was reflected in the following formulation on the proof copy of the *Short Biography* of Stalin:

> A commission of the Central Committee, All-Union Communist Party (Bolsheviks), under the direction of Comrade Stalin and with his most active personal participation, prepared a *Short Course of the History of the All-Union Communist Party (Bolsheviks)*.

But even this phrase did not satisfy Stalin; the following sentence replaced it in the final version of the *Short Biography:*

'In 1938 appeared the book, *History of the All-Union Communist Party (Bolsheviks), Short Course,* written by Comrade Stalin and approved by a commission of the Central Committee, All-Union Communist Party (Bolsheviks).' Can one add anything more? (*Animation in the hall.*)

As you see, a surprising metamorphosis changed a work created by a group into a book written by Stalin. It is not necessary to state how and why this metamorphosis took place.

A pertinent question comes to our mind: If Stalin is the author of this book, why did he need to praise the person of Stalin so much and to transform the whole post-October [1917] historical period our glorious Communist Party solely into an action of 'the Stalin genius'?

Did this book properly reflect the efforts of the party in the socialist transformation of the country, in the construction of socialist society, in the industrialization and collectivization of the country, and also other steps taken by the party which undeviatingly travelled the path outlined by Lenin? This book speaks principally about Stalin, about his speeches, about his reports. Everything without the smallest exception is tied to his name.

And when Stalin himself asserts that he himself wrote the *Short Course of the History of the All-Union Communist Party (Bolsheviks)*, this calls at least for amazement. Can a Marxist-

Leninist thus write about himself, praising his own person to the heavens?

Or let us take the matter of the Stalin Prizes. (*Movement in the hall.*) Not even the tsars created prizes which they named after themselves.

Stalin recognized as the best a text of the national anthem of the Soviet Union which contains not a word about the communist party; it contains, however, the following unprecedented praise of Stalin:

> Stalin brought us up in loyalty to the people,
> He inspired us to great toil and acts.

In these lines of the anthem the whole educational, directional and inspirational activity of the great Leninist party is ascribed to Stalin. This is, of course, a clear deviation from Marxism-Leninism, a clear debasing and belittling of the role of the party. We should add for your information that the Presidium of the Central Committee has already passed a resolution concerning the composition of a new text of the anthem, which will reflect the role of the people, and the role of the party. (*Loud, prolonged applause.*)

And was it without Stalin's knowledge that many of the largest enterprises and towns were named after him? Was it without his knowledge that Stalin monuments were erected throughout the country — these 'memorials to the living'? It is a fact that Stalin himself signed on July 2, 1951, a resolution of the U.S.S.R. Council of Ministers concerning the erection on the Volga-Don Canal of an impressive monument to Stalin; on September 4 of the same year he issued an order making 33 tons of copper available for the construction of this impressive monument. Anyone who has visited the Stalingrad area must have seen the huge statue which is being built there, and that on a site which hardly any people frequent. Huge sums were spent to build it at a time when people of this area had lived since the war in huts. Consider yourself, was Stalin right when he wrote in his biography that ' . . . he did not allow in himself . . . even a shadow of conceit, pride, or self-adoration'?

At the same time Stalin gave proofs of his lack of respect for Lenin's memory. It is no coincidence that, despite the decision taken over 30 years ago to build a Palace of Soviets as a monument to Vladimir Ilyich, this Palace was not built, its construction was always postponed, and the project allowed to lapse.[36]

We cannot forget to recall the Soviet government resolution of August 14, 1925, concerning 'the founding of Lenin Prizes for educational work'. This resolution was published in the press, but until this day there are no Lenin Prizes. This, too, should be corrected. (*Tumultuous, prolonged applause.*)

During Stalin's life, thanks to known methods which I have mentioned, and quoting facts, for instance, from the *Short Biography* of Stalin — all events were explained as if Lenin played only a secondary role, even during the October Socialist Revolution. In many films and in many literary works, the figure of Lenin was incorrectly presented and inadmissibly belittled.

Stalin loved to see the film, 'The Unforgettable Year of 1919', in which he was shown on the steps of an armored train and where he was practically vanquishing the foe with his own sabre. Let Kliment Yefremovich [Voroshilov] our dear friend, find the necessary courage and write the truth about Stalin; after all, he knows how Stalin fought. It will be difficult for Comrade Voroshilov to undertake this, but it would be good if he did it. Everyone will approve of it, both the people and the party. Even his grandsons will thank him. (*Prolonged applause.*)

In speaking about the events of the October Revolution and about the Civil War, the impression was created that Stalin always played the main role, as if everywhere and always Stalin had suggested to Lenin what to do and how to do it. However, this is slander of Lenin. (*Prolonged applause.*)

I will probably not sin against the truth when I say that 99 percent of the persons present here heard and knew very little about Stalin before the year 1924, while Lenin was known to all; he was known to the whole party, to the whole nation, from the children up to the greybeards. (*Tumultuous, prolonged applause.*)

All this has to be thoroughly revised, so that history, literature, and the fine arts properly reflect V. I. Lenin's role and the great deeds of our Communist Party and of the Soviet people — the creative people. (*Applause.*)

Comrades! The cult of the individual caused the employment of faulty principles in party work and in economic activity; it brought about crude violation of internal party and soviet democracy, sterile administration, deviations of all sorts, covering up of shortcomings and varnishing of reality. Our nation gave birth to many flatterers and specialists in false optimism and deceit.

We should also not forget that due to the numerous arrests of party, soviet and economic leaders, many workers began to work uncertainly, showed over-cautiousness, feared all that was new, feared their own shadows and began to show less initiative in their work.

Take, for instance, party and soviet resolutions. They were prepared in a routine manner often without considering the concrete situation. This went so far that party workers, even during the smallest sessions, read their speeches. All this produced the danger of formalizing party and soviet work and of bureaucratizing the whole apparatus.

Stalin's reluctance to consider life's realities and the fact that he was not aware of the real state of affairs in the provinces can be illustrated by his direction of agriculture.

All those who interested themselves even a little in the national situation saw the difficult situation in agriculture, but Stalin never even noted it. Did we tell Stalin about this? Yes, we told him, but he did not support us. Why? Because Stalin never traveled anywhere, did not meet city and kolkhoz workers; he did not know the actual situation in the provinces.

He knew the country and agriculture only from films. And these films had dressed up and beautified the existing situation in agriculture.

Many films so pictured kolkhoz life that the tables were bending from the weight of turkeys and geese. Evidently Stalin thought that it was actually so.

Vladimir Ilyich Lenin looked at life differently; he was always close to the people; he used to receive peasant delegates, and often spoke at factory gatherings; he used to visit villages and talk with the peasants.

Stalin separated himself from the people and never went anywhere. This lasted for decades. The last time he visited a village was in January 1928 when he visited Siberia in connection with grain deliveries. How then could he have known the situation in the provinces?

And when he was once told during a discussion that our situation on the land was a difficult one and that the situation of stockraising and meat production was especially bad, a commission was formed which was charged with the preparation of a resolution called, 'Means towards further development of stockraising in kolkhozes and sovkhozes'. We worked out this project.[37]

Of course, our propositions of that time did not contain all possibilities, but we did charter ways in which stockraising on the kolkhozes and sovkhozes would be raised. We proposed then to raise the prices of such products in order to create material incentives for the kolkhoz, MTS and sovkhoz workers in the development of cattle breeding. But our project was not accepted and in February 1953 was laid aside entirely.

What is more, while reviewing this project Stalin proposed that the taxes paid by the kolkhozes and by the kolkhoz workers should be raised by 40 thousand million rubles; according to him the peasants were well-off and the kolkhoz worker would need to sell only one more chicken to pay his tax in full.

Imagine what this meant. Certainly 40 thousand million rubles is a sum which the kolkhoz workers did not realize for all the products which they sold to the government. In 1952, for instance, the kolkhozes and the kolkhoz workers received 26,280 million rubles for all their products delivered and sold to the government.

Did Stalin's position then rest on data of any sort whatever? Of course not.

In such cases facts and figures did not interest him. If Stalin said anything, it meant it was so — after all, he was a 'genius' and a genius does not need to count, he only needs to look and can immediately tell how it should be. When he expresses his opinion, everyone has to repeat it and admire his wisdom.

But how much wisdom was contained in the proposal to raise the agricultural tax by 40 thousand million rubles? None, absolutely none, because the proposal was not based on an actual assessment of the situation but on the fantastic ideas of a person divorced from reality. We are currently beginning slowly to work our way out of a difficult agricultural situation. The speeches of the delegates to the 20th Congress please us all; we are glad that many delegates deliver speeches, that there are conditions for the fulfillment of the Sixth Five-Year Plan for animal husbandry, not during the period of five years, but within two to three years. We are certain that the commitments of the new Five-Year Plan will be fulfilled successfully. (*Prolonged applause.*)

Comrades! If we sharply criticize today the cult of the individual which was so widespread during Stalin's life and if we speak about the many negative phenomena generated by this cult which is so alien to the spirit of Marxism-Leninism, various persons may ask: How could it be? Stalin headed the party and the country for 30 years and many victories were gained during his lifetime. Can we deny this? In my opinion, the question can be asked in this manner only by those who are blinded and hopelessly hypnotized by the cult of the individual, only by those who do not understand the essence of the revolution and of the Soviet state, only by those who do not understand, in a Leninist manner, the role of the party and of the nation in the development of Soviet society.

The socialist revolution was attained by the working class and the poor peasants with the partial support of the middle peasants. It was attained by people under the leadership of the Bolshevik Party. Lenin's great service consisted of the fact that he created a militant party of the working class, but he was armed with Marxist understanding of the laws of social development and with the science of proletarian victory in the fight with capitalism, and he steeled this party in the crucible of revolutionary struggle of the masses of the people. During this fight the party consistently defended the interests of the people, became its experienced leader, and led the working masses to power, to the creation of the first socialist state.

You remember well the wise words of Lenin that the Soviet state is strong because of the awareness of the masses that history is created by the millions and tens of millions of people.

Our historical victories were attained thanks to the organizational work of the party, to the many provincial organizations, and to the self-sacrificing work of our great nation. These victories are the result of the great drive and activity of the nation and of the party as a whole; they are not at all the fruit of the leadership of Stalin, as the situation was pictured during the period of the cult of the individual.

If we are to consider this matter as Marxists and as Leninists, then we have to state unequivocally that the leadership practice which came into being during the last years of Stalin's life became a serious obstacle in the path of Soviet social development.

Stalin often failed for months to take up some unusually important problems concerning the life of the party and of the state whose solution could not be postponed. During Stalin's leadership our peaceful relations with other nations were often threatened, because one-man decisions could cause and often did cause great complications.

In recent years, when we have managed to free ourselves from the harmful practice of the cult of the individual and to take several proper steps in the sphere of internal and external policy, everyone has seen how activity grew before their very eyes, how the creative activity of the broad working masses has developed, how favorably all this has acted upon the development of economy, and of culture. (*Applause*.)

Some comrades may ask us: Where were the members of the Political Bureau of the Central Committee? Why did they not assert themselves against the cult of the individual in time? And why is this being done only now?

First of all we have to consider the fact that the members of the Political Bureau viewed these matters in a different way at different times. Initially, many of them backed Stalin actively because Stalin was one of the strongest Marxists and his logic, his strength and his will greatly influenced the cadres and party work.

It is known that Stalin, after Lenin's death, especially during the first years, actively fought for Leninism against the enemies of Leninist theory and against those who deviated. Beginning with Leninist theory, the party, headed by its Central Committee, started on a great scale the work of socialist industrialization of the country, agricultural collectivization and the cultural revolution. At that time Stalin gained great popularity, sympathy and support. The party had to fight those who attempted to lead the country away from the correct Leninist path; it had to fight Trotskyites, Zinovievites and rightists, and the bourgeois nationalists. This fight was indispensable. Later, however, Stalin, abusing his power more and more, began to fight eminent party and government leaders and to use terroristic methods against honest Soviet people. As we have already shown, Stalin treated in this way such eminent party and government leaders as Kosior, Rudzutak, Eikhe, Postyshev and many others.

Attempts to oppose groundless suspicions and charges resulted in the opponent falling victim of the repression. This characterized the fall of Comrade Postyshev.

In one of his speeches Stalin expressed his dissatisfaction with Postyshev and asked him, 'What are you actually?'

Postyshev answered clearly, 'I am a Bolshevik, Comrade Stalin, a Bolshevik.'

This assertion was at first considered to show a lack of respect for Stalin; later it was considered a harmful act and consequently resulted in Postyshev's liquidation and branding without any reason as an 'enemy of the people'.

In the situation which then prevailed I often talked with Nikolai Alexandrovich Bulganin; once when we two were traveling in a car, he said, 'It has happened sometimes that a man goes to Stalin on his invitation as a friend. And when he sits with Stalin, he does not know where he will be sent next, home or to jail'.

It is clear that such conditions put every member of the Political Bureau in a very difficult situation. And when we also consider the fact that in the last years plenary sessions of the Central Committee were not convened and the sessions of the Political Bureau occurred only occasionally, from time to time, then we will understand how difficult it was for any member of the Political Bureau to take a stand against one or another unjust or improper procedure, against serious errors and shortcomings in the practices of leadership.

As we have already shown, many decisions were taken either by one person or in a roundabout way, without collective discussions. The sad fate of Political Bureau member, Comrade Voznesensky, who fell victim to Stalin's repressions, is known to all. It is a characteristic thing that the decision to remove him from the Political Bureau was never discussed but was reached in a devious fashion. In the same way came the decision concerning the removal of Kuznetsov and Rodionov from their posts.[38]

The importance of the Central Committee's Political Bureau was reduced and its work was disorganized by the creation within the Political Bureau of various commissions — the so-called 'fives', 'sixes', 'sevens' and 'nines'. Here is, for instance, a resolution of the Political Bureau of October 3, 1946.

Stalin's Proposal:

1. The Political Bureau Commission for Foreign Affairs ('the Six') is to concern itself in the future, in addition to foreign affairs, also with matters of internal construction and domestic policy.

2. The 'Six' is to add to its roster the Chairman of the State Planning Commission [of the Council of Ministers] of the U.S.S.R., Comrade Voznesensky, and is to be known as 'the Seven'.
   Signed: Secretary of the Central Committee, J. Stalin.

What a card player's terminology! (*Laughter in the hall.*) It is clear that the creation within the Political Bureau of this type of commission — 'fives', 'sixes', 'sevens' and 'nines' — was against the principle of collective leadership. The result of this was that some members of the Political Bureau were in this way kept away from participation in reaching the most important state matters.

One of the oldest members of our party, Kliment Yefremovich Voroshilov, found himself in an almost impossible situation. For several years he was actually deprived of the right of participation in Political Bureau sessions. Stalin forbade him to attend the Political Bureau sessions and to receive documents. When the Political Bureau was in session and Comrade Voroshilov heard about it, he telephoned each time and asked whether he would be allowed to attend. Sometimes Stalin permitted it, but always showed his dissatisfaction. Because of his extreme suspicion, Stalin toyed also with the absurd and ridiculous suspicion that Voroshilov was an English agent. (*Laughter in the hall.*) It's true — an English agent. A special tapping device was installed in his home to listen to what was said there. (*Indignation in the hall.*)

By unilateral decision Stalin also separated one other man from the work of the Political Bureau — Andrei Andreevich Andreev. This was one of the most unbridled acts of willfulness.

Let us consider the first plenary session of the Central Committee after the 19th Party Congress when Stalin, in his talk at the session, characterized Vyacheslav Mikhailovich Molotov and Anastas Ivanovich Mikoyan and suggested that these old workers of our party were guilty of some baseless charges. It is not excluded that had Stalin remained at the helm for another several months, Comrades Molotov and Mikoyan would probably not have delivered any speeches at this congress.

Stalin evidently had plans to finish off the old members of the Political Bureau. He often stated that Political Bureau members should be replaced by new ones.

His proposal after the 19th Congress concerning the selection of 25 persons to the Central Committee Presidium was aimed at the removal of the old Political Bureau members and the bringing in of less experienced persons so that these would extol him in all sorts of ways.[39]

We can assume that this was also a design for the future annihilation of the old Political Bureau members and in this way a cover for all of Stalin's shameful acts, the acts which we are now considering.

Comrades! In order not to repeat the errors of the past, the Central Committee has declared itself resolutely against the cult of the individual. We consider that Stalin was excessively extolled. However, in the past Stalin undoubtedly performed great services to the party, to the working class, and to the international workers' movement.

This question is complicated by the fact that all we have just been discussing was done during Stalin's life under his leadership and with his concurrence; here Stalin was convinced that this was necessary for the defense of the interests of the working classes against the plotting of enemies and the attacks of the imperialist camp. He saw this from the position of the interests of the working class, of the interests of the laboring people, of the interests of the victory of socialism and communism. We cannot say that these were the deeds of a giddy despot. He considered that this should be done in the interests of the party and of the working masses, in the name of the defense of the gains of the revolution. In this lies the whole tragedy!

Comrades! Lenin frequently stressed that modesty is an absolutely integral part of a real Bolshevik. Lenin himself was the living personification of the greatest modesty. We cannot say that we have been following this Leninist example in all respects. It is enough to point out that many towns, factories and industrial enterprises, kolkhozes and sovkhozes, soviet institutions and cultural institutions have been referred to by us with a title — if I may express it so — of private property of the names of these or those government or party leaders who were still active and in good health. Many of us participated in the action of assigning our names to various towns, raions [districts], undertakings and kolkhozes. We must correct this. (*Applause*.)

But this should be done calmly and slowly. The Central Committee will discuss this matter and consider it carefully in order to prevent errors and excesses. I can remember how the Ukraine learned about Kosior's arrest. The Kiev radio used to start its programs thus: 'This is radio [in the name of] Kosior'. When one day the programs began without naming Kosior, everyone was quite certain that something had happened to Kosior, that he probably had been arrested.

Thus, if today we begin to remove the signs everywhere and to change names, people will think that the comrades in whose honor the given enterprises, kolkhozes or cities are named, have also met some bad fate and that they have also been arrested. (*Animation in the hall.*)

How is the authority and the importance of this, or that leader judged? On the basis of how many towns, industrial enterprises and factories, kolkhozes and sovkhozes carry his name. Is it not about time we eliminated this 'private property' and 'nationalize' the factories, the industrial enterprises, the kolkhozes and the sovkhozes? (*Laughter, applause, voices: 'That is right'*.) This will benefit our cause. After all the cult of the individual is manifested also in this way.[40]

We should consider the question of the cult of the individual in all seriousness. We cannot let this matter get out of the party, especially not to the press. It is for this reason that we are considering it here at a closed congress session. We should know the limits; we should not give ammunition to the enemy; we should not wash our dirty linen before their eyes. I think that the delegates to the congress will understand and assess properly all these proposals. (*Tumultuous applause.*)

Comrades: We must abolish the cult of the individual decisively, once and for all; we must draw the proper conclusions concerning both ideological-theoretical and practical work.

It is necessary for this purpose:

First, in a Bolshevik manner to condemn and to eradicate the cult of the individual as alien to Marxism-Leninism and not consonant with the principles of party leadership and the norms of party life, and to fight inexorably all attempts at bringing back this practice in one form or another.

To return to and actually practice in all our ideological work the most important theses of Marxist-Leninist science about the people as the creator of history and as the creator of all material and spiritual good of humanity, about the decisive role of the Marxist party in the revolutionary fight for the transformation of society, about the victory of communism.

In this connection we will be forced to do much work in order to examine critically from the Marxist-Leninist viewpoint and to correct widely spread erroneous views connected with the cult of the individual in the sphere of history, philosophy, economics and other sciences, as well as in literature and the fine arts. It is especially necessary that in the immediate future we compile a serious textbook of the history of our party which will be edited in accordance with scientific Marxist objectivity, a textbook of the history of Soviet society, a book pertaining to the events of the Civil War and the Great Patriotic War.[41]

Secondly, to continue systematically and consistently the work done by the Party's Central Committee in the last few years, a work characterized by minute observation in all party organizations, from the bottom to the top, of the Leninist principles of party leadership, characterized, above all, by the main principle of collective leadership, characterized by the observation of the norms of party life described in the rules of our party, and finally, characterized by the wide practice of criticism and self-criticism.

Thirdly, to restore completely the Leninist principles of Soviet socialist democracy, expressed in the Constitution of the Soviet Union, to fight the arbitrariness of individuals who abuse their power. The evil caused by acts violating revolutionary socialist legality which have accumulated over a long period as a result of the negative influence of the cult of the individual has to be completely corrected.

Comrades! The 20th Congress of the Communist Party of the Soviet Union has manifested with a new strength the unshakable unity of our party, its cohesiveness around the Central Committee, its resolute will to accomplish the great task of building communism.(*Tumultuous applause.*) And the fact that we present in all their ramifications the basic problems of overcoming the cult of the individual which is alien to Marxism-Leninism, as well as the problem of liquidating its burdensome consequences, is evidence of the great moral and political strength of our party. (*Prolonged applause.*)

We are absolutely certain that our party, armed with the historical resolutions of the 20th Congress, will lead the Soviet people along the Leninist path to new successes, to new victories. (*Tumultuous, prolonged applause.*)

Long live the victorious banner of our party — Leninism! (*Tumultuous, prolonged applause ending in ovation. All rise.*)

NOTES

1. On the political significance of the 'full' Central Committee and its revival following the death of Stalin, *see* T. H. Rigby, 'Khrushchev and the Central Committee', *Australian Outlook*, September 1959, Vol. 13.

2. This letter as printed in the fifth edition of Lenin's *Sochineniia* (Collected Works) was marked '*strictly secret and personal.* Copy for comrades Kamenev and Zinoviev'.

3. These documents were distributed to 20th Congress delegates and to recipients of the present version of the report. The United States Department of State issued translations on 30 June 1956. They were subsequently published in the Soviet Union, and included in the fifth edition of Lenin's *Sochineniia*. On Lenin's 'testament', *see* Leonard Schapiro, *The Communist Party of the Soviet Union*, New York 1960, Ch. 15.

4. On Bukharin's policies and his defeat by Stalin, *see* Schapiro, *The Communist Party of the Soviet Union*, Ch. 20.

5. For a full and objective account of this incident, *see* Leonard Schapiro, *The Origin of the Communist Autocracy*, London 1955, pp. 59-62.

6. Here and elsewhere Khrushchev is concerned to exculpate himself (and other surviving members of Stalin's entourage) from responsibility for the purges of the later Stalin era, incriminating only Beria, Stalin's political police chief, who was arrested and executed in 1953. There is, however, reason to think that Beria was not the agent of some of Stalin's later machinations, and that Khrushchev, whether directly involved or not, stood to gain from them. *See* R. Conquest, *Power and Policy in the U.S.S.R.*, London 1961 and New York 1961, Chs 7-9.

7. This statement is contradicted by other Soviet sources, which claim that a plenary session of the Central Committee took place in January 1944. *See Pravda*, 28 January 1944, and *Kommunisticheskaia Partiia Sovetskogo Soiuza v rezoliutsiiakh i resheniiakh s"ezdov, konferentsii i plenumov TsK*, Moscow, Gospolitizdat, 1953, Chast' II, p. 1018.

8. Persons who had worked under Khrushchev when he was party boss of Moscow and later of the Ukraine during the 1930s must have received his protestations of indignation at the persecution of party officials during this period with some cynicism. Khrushchev's record as a hounder of 'enemies of the people' in these

years was unsurpassed by any of those who were now his col-
leagues in the Presidium. *See* Edward Crankshaw, *Khrushchev:
A Career*, New York 1966, Ch. 9.

9. Bertram Wolfe considers the word 'statistician' a translator's
error, due to confusion between the Russian words *statistik*
(statistician) and *statist* (actor with walk-on part). He suggests
that this passage should read ' . . . all he needed were people to fill
the stage'. (B. Wolfe, *Khrushchev and Stalin's Ghost*, pp. 84-5).
This interpretation is supported by what Khrushchev later says
about Stalin's lack of interest in facts and figures.

10. *See also* pp. 97-8, 111.

11. The Soviet political police organization was originally known as
the Cheka, from the Russian initials of its title. Subsequent re-
organizations involved the following confusing changes of nomen-
clature (we give conventional abbreviations only): GPU, OGPU,
NKVD, NKGB, MGB, MVD, KGB (this last since 1954). However, continuity is indicated by the appellation 'Chekist', still
applied to political police officers, usually when overtones of
approval are intended.

12. On the terror of 1936-8, *see* John A. Armstrong, *The Politics of
Totalitarianism*, New York 1961, Chs IV and V.

13. P. P. Postyshev (1888-1940), at that time Second Secretary of the
Ukrainian Central Committee and a Candidate Member of the
Politburo, was one of the most senior officials to fall victim to
the 1936-8 terror.

14. R. I. Eikhe (1890-1940), a candidate Member of the Politburo,
held senior party and government posts in Siberia.

15. Ya. E. Rudzutak (1887-1938) was a Full Member of the Politburo from 1926 to 1932, and re-entered it as a Candidate Member
in 1934. Prior to his arrest, he was chairman of the Central
Control Commission (the internal disciplinary machinery of the
CPSU).

16. The State Department translation has here 'the Collegium of the
Supreme Military Court', which is evidently an error.

17. S. V. Kosior (1889-1939), a Full Member of the Politburo, was
Khrushchev's predecessor as First Secretary of the Ukrainian
Central Committee — hence Khrushchev's obvious concern to de-
limit responsibility for his arrest.

18. V. Ya. Chubar (1891-1941) was a Candidate Member of the Politburo and Premier of the Ukraine.

19. A. V. Kosarev (1903-1939) was a member of the Orgburo of the Central Committee of the CPSU and General Secretary of the Komsomol (the Communist Youth League).

20. Beria succeeded Yezhov as head of the NKVD in November 1938, and Yezhov disappeared soon thereafter.

21. For the impact of the purges of the 1930s on the Soviet armed forces *see* John Erickson, *The Soviet High Command: A Military-Political History, 1918-1941*, London and New York, 1962, Chs XIV and XV, and John A. Armstrong, *The Politics of Totalitarianism*, pp. 61-4.

22. After World War II Stalin relegated Zhukov to the command of a provincial military district. On Stalin's death he was made First Deputy Minister of Defence and in 1955 Minister. At this period Khrushchev was clearly courting Zhukov's support, and was rewarded in June 1957 when Zhukov is thought to have assisted him against the 'anti-party group'. He now became a Full Member of the Central Committee Presidium. Khrushchev, however, was no less uneasy about the accumulation of power in the hands of a popular military leader than was Stalin, and in October 1957 he secured his removal as Defence Minister and Member of the Presidium.

23. A famous Cossack who performed heroic feats against the Germans in World War I.

24. A. N. Poskrebyshev, who was head of Stalin's personal secretariat for many years, disappeared after the dictator's death.

25. Apart from the peoples referred to here by Khrushchev, the Volga Germans and Crimean Tatars were also deported during World War II, and their Autonomous Republics were liquidated. Subsequent to the 20th Congress, the survivors among these deported nationalities, apart from the Volga Germans and Crimean Tatars, were returned to their native territories. *See* R. Conquest, *The Soviet Deportation of Nationalities*, London and New York, 1960.

26. The 'Leningrad affair' was basically a purge of the associates and protégés of Andrei Zhdanov, Central Committee Secretary and apparent contender for the succession to Stalin, following Zhdanov's death in August 1948. In this speech Khrushchev blames the fabrication of this affair on Beria and his henchmen,

but later Malenkov was to be implicated as well. *See* R. Conquest, *Power and Policy in the U.S.S.R.*, Ch. 5. At the time of their arrest N. A. Voznesensky (1903-50) was a Full Member of the Politburo and Deputy Premier in charge of planning, A. A. Kuznetsov (1905-49) was a Secretary of the Central Committee and member of the Orgburo, M. I. Rodionov was Premier of the Russian Republic (R.S.F.S.R.), and P. S. Popkov (1903-49) was First Secretary of the Leningrad Regional and City Committees of the CPSU.

27. A. S. Abakumov was MGB Minister from 1946 to 1951.

28. On the various purges and counter-purges in Georgia in 1951-2, *see* Conquest, *Power and Policy in the U.S.S.R.*, Ch. 7. There can be little doubt that, contrary to the impression given by Khrushchev, these events were due mainly to an attempt to weaken Beria's position in Georgia.

29. Until October 1952 the official title of the Soviet Communist Party was still 'All-Union Communist Party (Bolsheviks)'.

30. It is extremely doubtful whether Beria was involved in the fabrication of the 'doctors' plot' case, and probable that he was intended as one of the victims of the elaborate design of which this case and the 'Mingrelian nationalist case' were episodes. It is significant that Beria 'exploded' the 'doctors' plot' case after he regained control of the political police in 1953, whereas S. D. Ignatiev, who was in charge of the police at the time the 'plot' was 'discovered', did well under Khrushchev's patronage after Beria was arrested. *See* Conquest, *Power and Policy in the U.S.S.R.*, Chs 8 and 9.

31. Mussavat was a Muslim democratic party which achieved a leading position in the Azerbaidzhan Republic set up after the 1917 Revolution, until the reconquest of the Caucasus by the Bolsheviks.

32. 'Sergo' was a party nickname for G. K. Ordzhonikidze, a Georgian 'Old Bolshevik' who supported Stalin during the 1920s and became a Full Member of the Politburo in 1930.

33. M. S. Kedrov (1878-1941) played a prominent part in the Bolshevik underground and the 1917 Revolution, and subsequently occupied a number of senior party and government posts.

34. At the time Ordzhonikidze was officially stated to have died of a heart attack.

35. The passage omitted reads as follows: ' . . . consisting of Stalin, Molotov, Kalinin, Voroshilov, Kuibyshev, Frunze, Dzerzhinsky, Kaganovich, Ordzhonikidze, Kirov, Yaroslavsky, Mikoyan, Andreev, Shvernik, Zhdanov, Shkiriatov and others.' *See Joseph Stalin: A Short Biography*, Foreign Languages Publishing House, Moscow, 1949, p. 89.

36. It should be noted in Stalin's defence here that eleven years after these remarks of Khrushchev's there is still no Palace of Soviets, though there is a fine new congress hall in the Kremlin.

37. Khrushchev was probably the Politburo member most actively engaged in agricultural policy and administration during this period.

38. On Voznesensky, Kuznetsov and Rodionov, *see* Note. 26.

39. Following the 19th Congress in October 1952, the old Politburo of approximately a dozen members was abolished, giving way to a 'Presidium of the Central Committee' consisting of 25 full and 11 candidate members. As later transpired, there was also a 'Bureau' within the Presidium, but the size and membership of this body have never been revealed. Following Stalin's death, the Presidium was cut down to the size of the old Politburo, and in 1966 the title Politburo was finally restored.

40. This proposal was subsequently implemented. It is obvious that such leaders as Molotov, Voroshilov and Kaganovich, who had succeeded in having more places and institutions named after themselves, stood to lose more from this renaming operation than did Khrushchev himself.

41. A new *History of the Communist Party of the Soviet Union*, written by a group of party theoreticians and historians led by B. N. Ponomarev, appeared in 1959. This, with subsequent revisions, has remained the official party textbook.

Resolution of the 20th Congress
of the Communist Party of the Soviet Union
on Cde. N. S. Khrushchev's Report
'On the Cult of Personality and its Consequences'

EDITOR'S NOTE

From *XX s"ezd Kommunisticheskoi Partii Sovetskogo Soiuza: stenograficheskii otchët* (Stenographic Report of the 20th Congress of the CPSU), Vol. II, p. 498. Editor's translation. The peculiar formulation to the effect that the congress had heard Khrushchev's report and approved the propositions of that of the Central Committee has been interpreted by some observers as a compromise whereby those concerned (including Khrushchev's rivals in the leadership) were committed to the general lines of the critique of Stalin, but not to the gloss added by Khrushchev.

(Adopted unanimously on February 25, 1956)

Having heard Cde. N. S. Khrushchev's report on the cult of personality and its consequences, the 20th Congress of the Communist Party of the Soviet Union approves the propositions in the Central Committee's report and instructs the CC CPSU to consistently carry out measures to ensure the complete overcoming of the cult of personality, which is foreign to Marxism-Leninism, the elimination of its consequences from all fields of party, government and ideological work, and the strict application of the norms of party life and the principles of collectivity in party leadership, worked out by the great Lenin.

Khrushchev Returns to the Attack

Extracts from Khrushchev's Closing Remarks to
the Debate on the Report of the Central Committee
to the 22nd Congress of the CPSU, 27 October 1961.[1]

EDITOR'S NOTE

Having assumed at the 20th Congress the leadership of the attack
on Stalin, Khrushchev was obliged to defend that role when the
inevitable reaction came, and in so doing he became more and
more the prisoner of the role.

The first dramatic illustration of this was the 'anti-party group'
crisis of June 1957, when a majority in the ruling Presidium
voted to remove Khrushchev from the First Secretaryship, but
Khrushchev managed to get a plenary session of the Central
Committee to overrule this decision and expel his attackers from
the leadership.[2] The 'anti-party group' included the most diehard
Stalinists, and Khrushchev's handling of the attack on Stalin was
one of the issues in terms of which this struggle was fought. The
'de-Stalinizing' position on which Khrushchev won the encounter,
however, then set limits to the extent and the manner in which
he could exploit his victory. Since the 22nd Congress was the
first regular congress convened after this crisis (there was an
'extraordinary' congress in 1959 to deal with the new seven-
year plan), Khrushchev and others were obliged to refer to these
events, and to defend the position then taken.

Meanwhile, as the dispute and rivalry between the Soviet
Union and Communist China developed, the Chinese had been
seeking to rally to their side those elements in the international
communist movement who were disturbed by the Soviet position
on Stalin and his methods. By 1961 they had succeeded in this
way in detaching Albania from the Soviet Union, and the refusal
of the Albanian leadership to send representatives to the 22nd

CPSU Congress brought this out into the open.[3] This obliged Khrushchev to attack the Albanian leaders publicly (as well, by implication, as their Chinese mentors — provoking the Chinese representative Chou En-lai to demonstratively walk out). However, in order to justify this attack and thereby to vindicate his leadership, he was now forced to *publicly* condemn Stalin and his methods, which in 1956 he had done only behind closed doors, and to commit himself personally to abstain from arbitrary actions and flouting the views of other leaders.

In so doing, however, he further restricted his freedom to manoeuvre in the job of staying on top. His personal authority and organizational power were still very great, enabling him, some observers think, to defeat a strong challenge from his deputy in the party machine Frol Kozlov in the winter of 1962-3. His powers of decision-making and patronage were probably sufficient to prevent a regular opposition faction from emerging in the leadership and growing to the point where it could oust him. But in the absence of Stalinist police powers, he was unable to guarantee himself against removal in the event of something like a general revolt of the leadership against him. In October 1964, in the context of a series of failures of Khrushchev's internal and external policies and attempts on his part to retrieve his position by daring new policy initiatives pushed through without proper consultation, such a revolt did occur. Khrushchev reportedly defended himself vigorously in the full Central Committee, but this time, unlike in 1957, they deserted him. Ironically, having triumphed over his earlier rivals largely through espousing the cause of opposing arbitrary one-man rule, Khrushchev provided the first clear evidence of the victory of this cause only in his own downfall.

Why have the Albanian leaders launched a campaign against the decisions of the 20th Congress of our party? What do they find seditious in them?

Above all, the resolute condemnation of the Stalin cult and its harmful consequences is not to the liking of the Albanian leaders. They are displeased that we have resolutely denounced the arbitrary rule, the abuse of power from which many innocent people suffered, among them eminent representatives of the old guard who had been with Lenin in building the world's first proletarian state. The Albanian leaders cannot speak without vexation and malice of the fact that we have put an end for good to the situation where one man at his own pleasure arbitrarily decided all-important questions relating to the life of our party and country. (*Prolonged applause.*)

Stalin is no longer among the living, but we have thought it necessary to denounce the disgraceful methods of leadership that flourished in the circumstances of the Stalin cult. Our party is doing this to prevent phenomena of this sort from ever being repeated . . .

[Khrushchev went on to argue that the Albanian party leaders opposed the criticism of Stalin's methods of rule because they were still employing similar methods inside their own country. He then turned to the question of differences inside the CPSU.]

Many comrades who have spoken here have angrily condemned the anti-party subversive activity of the handful of factionalists led by Molotov, Kaganovich and Malenkov. Our whole party and the entire people have rejected these renegades who opposed everything new and who wished to restore the vicious methods that reigned under the cult of the individual. They wanted to return to those days, so difficult for our party and our country, when no one was insured against arbitrariness and repressions. Yes, Molotov and the others wanted precisely that.

We resolutely reject such methods of leadership, if I may be permitted to call them that. We stand and we shall continue to stand firmly on the position that intra-party affairs must be solved on the basis of Leninist norms, on the basis of the methods of persuasion and broad democracy. (*Applause.*) The party's strongest weapon is its ideology, the great teaching of Marxism-Leninism, which has brought many glorious victories to the party, to the Soviet people and to the whole international communist movement. (*Prolonged applause.*)

Is it possible for different opinions to appear in the party at various periods of its activity, especially during transitional stages? Yes, it is possible. What should be done, then, with those who express their own opinion, different from that of others? We stand for the application in such cases not of repressions but of Leninist methods of persuasion and explanation.

Let me recall the following episode from the history of our party. On the eve of October, in the decisive days when the question was whether the Great Socialist Revolution was or was not to be, Zinoviev and Kamenev spoke out in the press against the armed uprising planned by the party and revealed the plans of the Central Committee of the party of Bolsheviks to its enemies. This was a betrayal of the cause of the revolution.

Vladimir Ilyich Lenin unmasked Zinoviev and Kamenev and demanded their expulsion from the party. The subsequent development of the revolution fully confirmed the correctness of Lenin's policy of armed uprising. When Zinoviev and Kamenev later declared that they had been mistaken and admitted their guilt, Lenin showed great magnanimity toward them and himself raised the question of reinstating them in the party leadership.

Vladimir Ilyich firmly pursued the course of developing intra-party democracy. He based himself on the broad masses of communists and non-party people.

In the years following Lenin's death, the Leninist norms of party life were grossly distorted in the conditions of the Stalin cult. Stalin elevated limitations on intra-party and soviet democracy to the status of norms of intra-party and state life. He crudely violated the Leninist principles of leadership and committed acts of arbitrariness and abuse of power.

Stalin could look at a comrade sitting at the same table with him and say: 'Your eyes seem to be shifty today', after which it could be assumed that the comrade whose eyes were supposedly shifty was under suspicion.

Comrade delegates! I wish to tell the congress how the anti-party group reacted to the proposal that the question of abuse of power in the period of the cult of personality be placed before the 20th Party Congress.

Molotov, Kaganovich, Malenkov, Voroshilov and others categorically objected to this proposal. In answer to their objections they were told that if they continued to oppose the raising of this question, the delegates to the party congress would be asked to decide the matter. We had no doubt that the congress would favour discussion of the question. Only then did they agree, and the question of the cult of personality was presented to the 20th Party Congress. But even after the congress, the factionalists continued their struggle and obstructed in every possible way the clarification of the question of the abuse of power, fearing that their role as accomplices in the mass repressions would be brought to light.

The mass repressions began after the murder of Kirov. A great deal of effort is still necessary to properly determine who was guilty of his death. The more deeply we study the materials relating to Kirov's death, the more questions arise. It is noteworthy that Kirov's assassin had previously been twice arrested by the chekists near the Smolny, and that weapons had been found on him. But on both occasions, upon someone's instructions, he had been released. And this man was in the Smolny, armed, in the very corridor along which Kirov usually passed. And for some reason or other it happened that at the moment of the murder the chief of Kirov's bodyguard had fallen far behind S. M. Kirov, although his instructions forbade him to be so far away from the person he was guarding.

The following fact is also very strange. When the chief of Kirov's bodyguard was being driven to the interrogation — and he was to have been questioned by Stalin, Molotov and Voroshilov — on the way, as the driver of the vehicle later said, an accident was deliberately staged by those who were to bring the chief of the bodyguard to the interrogation. They reported that the chief of the bodyguard had died as a result of the accident, although in actual fact it turned out he had been killed by the persons escorting him.

Thus the man who guarded Kirov was killed. Then those who had killed him were shot. This was apparently not a coincidence but a premeditated crime. Who could have committed it? A painstaking study of this complex case is now under way.

It has turned out that the driver of the vehicle that was carrying the chief of S. M. Kirov's bodyguard to the interrogation is alive. He has said that as they were riding to the interrogation an NKVD man was sitting with him in the cab. The vehicle was a truck. (It is strange, of course, that this man was being driven to the interrogation in a truck, as if in this case no other vehicle could be found for the purpose. It seems that everything had been thought out in advance, down to the smallest detail.) Two other NKVD men were in the back of the truck with the chief of Kirov's bodyguard.

The driver went on to say that as they were driving down the street the man sitting next to him suddenly grabbed the wheel out of his hands and steered the truck straight at a building. The driver grabbed the steering wheel back and straightened out the truck, and they merely sideswiped the wall of the building. Later he was told that the chief of Kirov's bodyguard had been killed in this accident.

Why was he killed while none of the persons accompanying him was even injured? Why were both these NKVD men who were escorting the chief of Kirov's bodyguard later themselves shot? It means that someone needed to have them killed in order to cover up all traces.

There are still many, a great many, unclarified circumstances in this and other similar cases.[4]

Comrades! It is our duty to make a painstaking and comprehensive study of all such cases connected with the abuse of power. Time will pass, we shall die, we are all mortal, but as long as we continue to work we can and must find out many things and tell the truth to the party and the people. It is an obligation to do everything possible to establish the truth now, for the more time passes since these events, the more difficult will it become to re-establish the truth. It is now too late to bring the dead back to life, as the saying goes. But it is necessary that all this be recorded truthfully in the history of the party. This must be done so that phenomena of this sort can never be repeated in the future. (*Stormy, prolonged applause.*)

You can imagine how difficult it was to solve questions of this kind when the Presidium of the Central Committee included people who had themselves been guilty of the abuse of power, of mass repressions. They stubbornly resisted all measures aimed at exposing the cult of personality and then launched a struggle against the Central Committee, wishing to change the composition of its leadership, to change the Leninist policy of the party, the course laid down by the 20th Congress.

Naturally, they did not want to investigate cases of this sort. You have heard Comrade Shelepin's speech.[5] He told the congress many things, but needless to say he told by no means all that has now come to light. Thousands of completely innocent people perished, and each person is a whole story. Many party, government and military figures perished.

Of course, those people in the Presidium of the Central Committee who had been responsible for violations of legality and mass repressions resisted in every possible way the exposure of arbitrary acts in the period of the personality cult and then they launched an anti-party factionalist struggle against the leadership of the Central Committee, concentrating their fire primarily against me personally, as First Secretary of the Central Committee, inasmuch as it had fallen to me in the course of my responsibilities to raise these questions. It was necessary to accept blows to oneself and to reply to these blows. (*Stormy, prolonged applause.*)

The participants in the anti-party factionalist group hoped to seize leadership in the party and the country and to remove the comrades who were exposing the criminal actions committed in the period of the personality cult. The anti-party group wanted to place Molotov in the leadership. Then, of course, there would have been no exposures of these abuses of power.

Even after the 20th Congress had condemned the personality cult, the anti-party group did all in its power to prevent the exposure from going any further. Molotov said that in large matters there may be both bad things and good. He justified the actions that had taken place in the period of the personality cult and predicted that such actions are possible and that their repetition in the future is possible. Such was the course of the anti-party factionalist group. This is not a simple error. It is a calculated, criminal and adventurist position. They wanted to divert the party and the country from the Leninist path, they wanted to return to the policy and methods of leadership of the period of the personality cult. But they miscalculated. The Central Committee, our whole party and the entire Soviet people administered a decisive rebuff to the anti-party group and exposed and crushed the factionalists. (*Stormy, prolonged applause.*)

People have spoken here with pain about many innocent victims among outstanding party and government figures.

Such outstanding military commanders as Tukhachevsky, Yakir, Uborevich, Kork, Egorov, Eideman and others fell victim to the mass repressions. They had been worthy people of our army, especially Tukhachevsky, Yakir and Uborevich, who had been outstanding military leaders. Later Bliukher and other outstanding military commanders fell victim to the repressions.

A rather curious report once appeared in the foreign press to the effect that Hitler, in preparing the attack on our country, planted through his intelligence service a faked document indicating that Comrades Yakir and Tukhachevsky and others were agents of the German general staff. This 'document', allegedly secret, fell into the hands of President Benes of Czechoslovakia, who, apparently guided by good intentions, forwarded it to Stalin.

Yakir, Tukhachevsky and other comrades were arrested and then killed.[6]

Many splendid commanders and political workers of the Red Army were executed. Here among the delegates there are comrades — I do not wish to name them so as not to cause them pain — who spent many years in prison. They were 'persuaded' — persuaded by quite definite techniques — that they were either German or British of some other kind of spies. And several of them 'confessed'. Even in cases when such people were told that the accusation of espionage had been withdrawn, they themselves insisted on their previous testimony, because they believed it was better to stand on their false testimony in order to put an end as quickly as possible to their torments and to meet death as quickly as possible.

That is what the personality cult means! That was the meaning of the actions of Molotov and the others who wanted to restore the vicious practices of the period of the personality cult. It was to this that the anti-party group wanted to return the party; this is precisely the reason why the struggle against them was so bitter and difficult. Everyone understood what it meant.

I knew Comrade Yakir well. I knew Tukhachevsky too, but not as well as Yakir. In 1961, during a conference in Alma-Ata, his son, who works in Kazakhstan, came to see me. He asked me about his father. What could I tell him? When we investigated these cases in the Presidium of the Central Committee and received a report that neither Tukhachevsky nor Yakir nor Uborevich had been guilty of any crime against the party and the state, we asked Molotov, Kaganovich and Voroshilov:

'Are you for rehabilitating them?'

'Yes, we are for it', they answered.

'But it was you who executed these people', we told them indignantly. 'When were you acting according to your conscience, then or now?'

But they did not answer this question. And they will not answer it. You have heard the comments they wrote on letters received by Stalin. What can they say?

In his speech to the congress, Comrade Shelepin told you how these finest representatives of the communist party in the Red Army were killed. He also read Comrade Yakir's letter to Stalin and the recommendations on this letter. It should be said that at one time Yakir was highly esteemed by Stalin.

It may be added that when Yakir was shot he exclaimed: 'Long live the party, long live Stalin!'

He had so much faith in the party, so much faith in Stalin that he never permitted himself the thought that a deliberate injustice was being committed. He believed that certain enemies had wormed their way into the organs of the NKVD.

When Stalin was told how Yakir had behaved before his death, he cursed Yakir.

Let us recall Sergo Ordzhonikidze. I attended Ordzhonikidze's funeral. I believed what was said at the time, that he had died suddenly, because we knew he had a weak heart. Much later, after the war, I learned quite by accident that he had committed suicide. Sergo's brother had been arrested and shot. Comrade Ordzhonikidze saw that he could no longer work with Stalin, although previously he had been one of his closest friends. Ordzhonikidze held a high party post. Lenin had known and valued him, but circumstances had become such that Ordzhonikidze could no longer work normally, and in order to avoid clashing with Stalin and sharing the responsibility for his abuse of power, he decided to take his life.

The fate of Alyosha Svanidze, the brother of Stalin's first wife, who was less well known to the broad circles of our party, was also tragic. He had been an old Bolshevik, but Beria made it appear, through all kinds of machinations, that Svanidze had been planted near Stalin by the German intelligence service, although he was a very close friend of Stalin's. And Svanidze was shot. Before the execution, Svanidze was told that Stalin had said that if he asked for forgiveness he would be pardoned. When Stalin's words were repeated to Svanidze, he asked: 'What should I ask [forgiveness] for? I have committed no crime'. He was shot. After Svanidze's death, Stalin said: 'See how proud he is: he died without asking forgiveness'. The thought never occurred to him that Svanidze had been above all an honest man.

Thus many completely innocent people perished.

That is what the personality cult means. That is why we cannot show the slightest tolerance towards abuses of power.

Comrades! The Presidium of the Congress has received letters from old Bolsheviks in which they write that in the period of the cult of the individual outstanding party and state figures, such loyal Leninists as Comrades Chubar, Kosior, Rudzutak, Postyshev, Eikhe, Voznesensky, Kuznetsov and others, died guiltless.

The comrades propose that the memory of the outstanding party and state figures who fell victim to completely unjustified repressions in the period of the personality cult be perpetuated.

We believe this proposal to be a proper one. (*Stormy, prolonged applause.*) It would be advisable to charge the Central Committee that will be elected by the 22nd Party Congress with deciding this question positively. Perhaps a monument should be erected in Moscow to the memory of the comrades who fell victim to arbitrary rule. (*Applause.*)

In the conditions of the personality cult the party was deprived of normal life. People who usurp power cease being accountable to the party, they escape from under its control. Herein is the greatest danger of the cult of the individual.

The situation in the party must always be such that every leader is accountable to the party and its agencies, that the party can replace any leader when it considers it necessary. (*Applause.*)

Now, since the 20th Congress, Leninist principles of party life and collective leadership have been restored in the party. The new Party Programme and Rules give legal force to propositions that restore the Leninist norms of party life and preclude the possibility of relapses into the personality cult.

The 20th Congress of our party condemned the personality cult, restored justice and demanded that the distortions that had taken place be eliminated. The Central Committee of the Party adopted resolute measures to prevent a return to arbitrariness and lawlessness. The anti-party group of Molotov, Kaganovich, Malenkov and others resisted in every possible way the implementation of these measures.

The factionalists undertook an attempt to seize the leadership and to turn the party away from the Leninist path. They prepared reprisals against those who had defended the course set by the 20th Congress. When the anti-party group was crushed, its participants expected that they would be treated in the same way that they had dealt with people at the time of the personality cult and in the way they hoped to deal with those who favoured the restoration of the Leninist norms of party life.

Typical was the conversation I had with Kaganovich. This was two days after the end of the June plenary session of the party Central Committee, which expelled the anti-party group from the Central Committee. Kaganovich called me on the telephone and said:

'Comrade Khrushchev, I have known you for many years. I ask you not to let them treat me in the way people were vindictively treated under Stalin'.

And Kaganovich knew how people had been treated because he himself had been a participant in these reprisals.

I answered him:

'Comrade Kaganovich! Your words once more confirm the methods you intended to use to achieve your disgusting ends. You wanted to return the country to the state of affairs that existed under the personality cult, you wanted to indulge in reprisals against people. And you measure other people by your own yardstick. But you are mistaken. We firmly observe and we shall adhere to Leninist principles. You will be given a job', I said to Kaganovich, 'you will be able to work and live in tranquility if you work honestly, as all Soviet people work'.

Such is the conversation I had with Kaganovich. This conversation shows that when the factionalists failed, they thought they would be dealt with in the same way that they intended to deal with the party cadres if they succeeded in realizing their crafty designs. But we Communists-Leninists cannot embark on the path of abuse of power. We stand firmly on party, Leninist positions, we believe in the strength and unity of our party and in the solidarity of the people around the party. (*Stormy applause.*) . . .

Comrades! The 22nd Congress has confirmed with full force that the course of the 20th Party Congress, the course of the restoration and further development of Leninist norms of party and state life, the course of raising the leading role of the party and the creative activity of the masses of the people, is the only correct course. The 22nd Congress confirms this beneficial course. The Party Programme and Rules and the resolutions of the congress set forth new guarantees against relapses into the personality cult. The role of the party as the great inspiring and organizing force in the building of communism is rising higher still.

I would like to say a few words about the following question. In many speeches at the congress, and not infrequently in our press as well, when mention is made of the activity of our party's Central Committee a certain special emphasis is placed on me personally, and my role in carrying out major party and government measures is emphasized.

I understand the kind feelings guiding these comrades. Allow me, however, to emphasize with full force that everything that is said about me should be said about the Central Committee of our Leninist party and about the Presidium of the Central Committee. (*Stormy, prolonged applause.*) Not one major measure, not one responsible pronouncement has been carried out upon anyone's personal directive; they have all been the result of collective discussion and collective decision. (*Stormy applause.*) And this concluding speech, too, has been considered and approved by the executive collective. (*Prolonged applause.*) Our great strength, comrades, lies in collective leadership, in collegial decisions on all questions of principle. (*Stormy applause.*)

No matter what abilities this or that leader may possess, no matter what contributions he may make to the cause, he cannot achieve true and lasting success without the support of the collective, without the most active participation of the whole party and of the broad popular masses in the implementation of adopted measures. This must be clearly understood and constantly borne in mind by all. (*Applause.*)

Communist leaders are strong through the activity of the masses they lead. If they correctly understand and express the interests of the party, the interests of the people, if they struggle for these interests without sparing their strength, their energy and even their life, if they are inseparable from the party in great matters and in small, just as the party is inseparable from the people, such leaders will always be supported by the party and the people. And the cause for which such a leader fights will inevitably triumph. (*Prolonged applause.*)

Of course, one must possess the qualities necessary for the struggle for the cause of the party and for the vital interests of the people. After all, our ideological opponents, our enemies concentrate their fire in the first place against those leaders who, rallying the *aktiv*[7] and through the *aktiv* the whole people around the leading organs, guide the cause along the only correct, Leninist path.

Here at the congress much has been said, for instance, about the furious energy employed by the anti-party factionalists Molotov, Kaganovich, Malenkov and others against the Leninist Central Committee of the Party and against me personally. Speaking against the course set forth by the 20th Congress, the splitters concentrated their main fire against Khrushchev, who was a nuisance to them. Why against Khrushchev? Well, because Khrushchev had been promoted by the will of the party to the post of First Secretary of the Central Committee. The factionalists badly miscalculated. The party ousted them both ideologically and organizationally. (*Stormy applause.*)

The Central Committee of our party displayed exceptionally high political maturity and a truly Leninist understanding of the situation. It is characteristic that literally not one full or candidate member of the Central Committee and not one member of the Revision Commission supported the miserable handful of splitters. (*Prolonged applause.*)

While resolutely pronouncing themselves opposed to all the disgusting phenomena of the personality cult, Marxist-Leninists have always recognized and will continue to recognize the authority of leaders.

But it would be incorrect to single out this or that leader, to set him apart from the leading collective or to exalt him inordinately. This is contrary to the principles of Marxism-Leninism. It is known with what impatience Marx, Engels and Lenin spoke out against those who eulogized their contributions. Yet it is difficult to overestimate the great role of the founders of scientific communism, Marx, Engels and Lenin, and their contributions to the working class and to all mankind. (*Prolonged applause.*)[8]

Feelings of self-praise and any special emphasis on, or excessive exaggeration of, the role of individual leaders are utterly alien to true Marxist-Leninists. They find it simply insulting when someone tries obtrusively to set them apart, to isolate them from the executive nucleus of comrades. (*Stormy applause.*)

We communists highly value and support the authority of correct and mature leadership. We must safeguard the authority of the leaders who are recognized by the party and the people. But every leader must also understand the other side of the matter — never to plume himself on his position, to remember that in holding this or that post he is merely fulfilling the will of the party and the will of the people, who may have invested him with the greatest power but never lose control over him. (*Applause.*) The leader who forgets this pays heavily for his mistake. I would add that he will pay while he is alive, or alternatively even after his death the people will not forgive him as has happened with the condemnation of the cult of Stalin.

(*Applause.*) A person who forgets that he is obliged to fulfil the will of the party and of the people cannot, properly speaking, be called a true leader; there must be no such 'leaders' either in the party or in the state apparatus. (*Applause.*)

Of course, for many reasons great power is concentrated in the hands of the man who holds a leading post. A leader advanced by the party and the people must not abuse his power. In the reports to the congress you have heard about the measures that we have implemented and that we shall carry out in order that a revival of the ugly phenomena of the cult of the individual may never recur in the future. But there is one thing that no statutory provision can prescribe: The collective of leaders must thoroughly understand that a situation must not be permitted to arise whereby any authority, even the most deserving one, can cease to take account of the opinions of those who have advanced him. (*Applause.*)

It is wrong, comrades, it is simply impossible to permit the inception and development of instances when the merited prestige of an individual may assume forms in which he gets it into his head that everything is permissible for him and that he no longer has need of the collective. In such a case this individual may stop listening to the voices of other comrades who have been advanced to leadership, just as he was, and may begin suppressing them. Our great teacher V. I. Lenin resolutely fought against this, and the party paid too dear a price for not heeding his wise counsel in good time.[9]

So let us be worthy disciples of Lenin in this important matter. (*Stormy, prolonged applause.*)

NOTES

1. *XXII s"ezd Kommunisticheskoi Partii Sovetskogo Soiuza: stenograficheskii otchët* (Stenographic Report of the 22nd Congress of the CPSU), Moscow, Gospolitizdat, 1962, Vol. II, pp. 579, 582-93. Editor's translation.

2. *See* Conquest, *Power and Policy in the U.S.S.R.*, Ch. 12.

3. On the role and consequences of the 22nd Congress and Khrushchev's attack on Albania in the Sino-Soviet dispute, *see* Alexander Dallin, with Jonathan Harris and Grey Hodnett (eds), *Diversity in International Communism: A Documentary Record, 1961-1963*, New York and London, 1963.

4. This account of Kirov's murder amplifies but otherwise parallels what Khrushchev said about it at the 20th Congress (see pp. 38-9). This and other parallels between the two speeches provide further evidence (if any were needed) for the authenticity of the State Department version of the 20th Congress speech.

5. A. N. Shelepin, then Chairman of the State Security Committee, cited a number of examples illustrating the cynical and callous attitude of Stalin, Molotov, Malenkov, Kaganovich and Voroshilov towards leading communists under sentence of death on fabricated charges. While Khrushchev's own public statements during the purge period seem to reveal a no less cynical attitude (*see* Crankshaw, *Khrushchev: A Career*, Ch. 9), he could fairly claim that he was not one of the inner circle conducting the purge.

6. The evidence on this incident, however, suggests that the data used by the Gestapo were originally supplied by Stalin's agents. *See* Armstrong, *The Politics of Totalitarianism*, p. 63 and *Survey: A Journal of Soviet and East European Affairs*, No. 63, April 1967, p. 176.

7. At each level of the hierarchy — national, regional, city, etc., those party members holding leading positions in the administrative, economic, cultural, military and all other fields are known as the *aktiv* of the party at that level.

8. Note how Khrushchev balances his condemnation of the tendencies towards a Khrushchev 'personality cult' with the implied claim to outstanding qualities of leadership warranting his enjoyment of great 'authority'.

9. This lesson was to be read back to Khrushchev after his removal in October 1964. The Central Committee journal *Party Life*, in a passage whose context identifies it clearly as referring to Khrushchev, though he was not directly named, declared as follows: 'Experienced and influential leaders who know their job enjoy deserved authority amongst us. People willingly listen to their voice and take account of their opinions, and this is an important condition of discipline, efficiency and success in executing the directives of the party. But legitimate respect has nothing in common with excessive extolling and eulogizing of a leader, such that every word of the man "on top" is given out as a revelation, and his steps and actions are regarded as infallible. Such an approach can lead to no good, it can only revive the habits of the personality cult period, and the party is irreconcilable to that. Every one of our organizations should be guided by the directives of the 20th, 21st and 22nd Congresses of the CPSU.

'The 22nd Congress wrote into the Party Rules: "The personality cult and the violations of intra-party democracy connected with it cannot be tolerated in the party, they are irreconcilable with the Leninist principles of party life". The consistent carrying out by the CPSU Central Committee of measures aimed at the complete overcoming of the pernicious consequences of the personality cult have been supported enthusiastically by all communists. But life shows that not all comrades have fully overcome the devices, forms and methods of work which became established in the period of the cult and have been rejected by life. It is precisely for this reason that the party is so insistent in questions of the observation of the principle of collective leadership and Leninist norms of party life in all echelons of the party and state apparatus. Not a single communist, not a single party collective, has the right to overlook cases where someone manifests conceit and stops taking notice of the opinions of his comrades, does not bother about the encouragement of criticism or about a creative and not just formal discussion of issues at plenary sessions, meetings and sittings [the term used here, *zasedaniia*, most often refers to the meetings of executive bodies]. One cannot permit even the most authoritative person to escape from control by the leading collective and the party organization, and to get the idea that he knows everything and can do everything, that he has no need of the knowledge and experience of his comrades. Every collective should be utterly uncompromising and insistent in this manner and should know how to check a man who goes too far'. (*Partiinaia zhizn'* [*Party Life*], No. 20, October, 1964, pp. 6-7.) The need for control 'from below' was said to apply to all officials, from the factory director and primary party organization secretary to 'the state and party leader of the very highest rank', and the Party's Central Committee and its Presidium were cited as an example of successful 'mutual control'.

A 17th Congress Delegate on the Proposal to Replace Stalin and the Murder of Kirov

EDITOR'S NOTE

By 1930 Stalin had defeated the last of the 'opposition' groupings and replaced them with his own supporters. He was still dissatisfied, however, and sought increased powers of repression in order to consolidate his personal dictatorship. Speaking to Boris Nicolaevsky in Paris in 1936, the former 'right opposition' leader Nikolai Bukharin stated that at this point Stalin began to encounter resistance amongst leading officials who had followed him faithfully through all the struggles of the 1920s, and that Kirov now emerged as the focus of a move towards less repressive, more consumer-oriented policies. Bukharin linked this with Kirov's murder and the subsequent party purge which was then beginning. (*See* Boris I. Nicolaevsky, *Power and the Soviet Elite*, pp. 26-65). Until 1964, when *Pravda* published the article abstracted below, there was no 'official' Soviet confirmation of any of this. L. Shaumyan, a delegate to the 17th Party Congress in 1934 which serves as the ostensible subject of his article, refers here to a move to remove Stalin from the General Secretaryship and clearly hints at the intention to replace him by Kirov.[1]

The Communist Party came to its 17th Congress united and monolithic.[2] Penitent speeches and acknowledgements of the party's successes were made at the congress by the former leaders of opposition groupings, Zinoviev, Kamenev, Bukharin, Rykov and Tomsky . . .

The 17th Congress entered the history of the CPSU as the congress of victors, as the congress which established the firm and irreversible victory of socialist relationships in our country and defined perspectives for the further advance of the Soviet people along the path to communism.

All that was the result of the consistent fulfilment of the designs of the great Lenin, the fruits of the heroic labour of Soviet people, who believed wholeheartedly in the party and its Central Committee. To the applause of the whole assembly N. S. Khrushchev declared:

> The strength of our Leninist Central Committee lies in the fact that it has managed to organize our party, has managed to organize our working class and collective farmers, and to direct their will and their energies to the reconstruction of our country and to the building of socialism in the U.S.S.R.

The congress delegates were people who had borne the brunt of the struggle for the building of the new social order, for the creation of Soviet industry, a socialist agriculture, and a new culture. One after another they mounted the Kremlin rostrum, shared their experience, and recounted their plans . . .

[Shaumyan went on to refer to the contribution made to the congress proceedings by some 30 party leaders, occupying the chief posts in various fields of activity — practically all of whom were soon to fall victim to Stalin's vengeance] . . . It was not for nothing that A. Yenukidze stated from the rostrum that in the [congress] hall were 'to be found all that is best in our party, all that is best in our country'.

By this time the cult of Stalin's personality had already begun to form. Departing ever farther from the Leninist norms of party life, Stalin cut himself off more and more from the masses, trampled on the principles of collective leadership, and abused his position. The abnormal state of affairs that was emerging in connection with the personality cult evoked alarm in many communists. Amongst certain congress delegates, as has subsequently transpired, and particularly amongst those who remembered well Lenin's testament,[3] the idea was maturing that the time had come to transfer Stalin from the post of General Secretary to some other job. This could not fail to reach Stalin's ears. He knew that in his efforts to further strengthen his position and to concentrate more personal power in his hands, he would encounter a decisive obstacle in the old Leninist cadres of the party. That fine Leninist, the darling of the whole party,

S. M. Kirov, referring to the successes in building socialism in the U.S.S.R., declared at this congress:

> If one recalls the path that preceded this victory of ours, then it becomes clear what an exceptional role has been played by our party, what an exceptional struggle the working class has borne under the leadership of our party in the cause of realizing Lenin's plan of building socialism in our country . . .

> Our successes are indeed enormous. The devil only knows, to use plain language, one feels such an urge to live and live, really, just look at what is being achieved and that is a fact![4]

But a year had not passed after the close of the 17th Congress, before a criminal hand cut short the life of Kirov. This was a crime thought out in advance and meticulously prepared, the circumstances of which, as N. S. Khrushchev made known at the 22nd Congress, are still not fully clarified.

The villainous murder of Kirov had dire effects on the life of the party and the state. Stalin employed this murder as a pretext for taking a harsh revenge on all persons inconvenient to him. The mass repressions began, and in the first instance a considerable proportion of the delegates to the 17th Party Congress were eliminated. Of the 1,966 delegates 1,108 were destroyed; of the 139 full and candidate members of the CC, elected at the 17th Congress, 98 persons perished, or 70 percent of the CC. A dire and unjustified blow had been struck at the old Leninist guard. Stalin had cleared the way for the further strengthening of the personality cult.

NOTES

1. Extracts taken from L. Shaumyan, 'Na rubezhe pervykh piatiletok: K 30-letiiu XVII s"ezda partii' ('On the Front Line of the First Five Year Plans: the 30th Anniversary of the 17th Party Congress'), *Pravda*, 7 February 1964. Editor's translation. L. Shaumyan is believed to be a close relative of S. G. Shaumyan, a prominent underground Bolshevik leader in the Caucasus, who was one of the '26 commissars' shot in 1918 allegedly by order of British officers.

2. For accounts of the historical context of the 17th Congress and its aftermath, *see* Schapiro, *The Communist Party of the Soviet Union*, Chs 21 and 22, and Armstrong, *The Politics of Totalitarianism*, Chs I and II.

3. *See* p. 26.

4. Here Kirov is developing his line that the party and the people, having suffered untold hardships to create a socialist order, should be treated with trust **an**d given the chance to enjoy the fruits of their achievements and to 'live'. Bukharin reported to Nicolaevsky that Kirov's speech at the congress was wildly cheered, the entire assembly rising to its feet, giving rise to discussion among delegates as to who received the most tumultuous reception, Kirov or Stalin. *See* Nicolaevsky, *Power and the Soviet Elite*, p. 35.

A Case History in Soviet Decision-Making under Stalin

Extract from the Memoirs of B. L. Vannikov
People's Commissar for Armaments.[1]

EDITOR'S NOTE

In his 'personality cult' speech Khrushchev revealed something of the devices and internal arrangements through which the top decision-making mechanism functioned under Stalin (*see* pp.80, 81). Milovan Djilas, in his *Conversations with Stalin* (Harcourt, Brace and World, Inc., New York, 1962, and Harmondsworth, Penguin Books, 1963) has given a vivid picture of the nocturnal gatherings at Stalin's dacha near Moscow, at which the dictator and his 'closest comrades-in-arms' settled pressing issues of state in the course of feasting and drinking. In the memoirs excerpted below we are given a unique glimpse of how the decision-making process appeared to those officials at the next level down, the members of the Council of People's Commissars. It reveals the complete dependence of these top administrators on the will of the inner leadership, and something of the process whereby the whim of Stalin was translated into a party-government decision. Vannikov is concerned here to show that Stalin's system of rule led not only to inhumanity, but also to inefficiency, that it made for decisions which were — in both senses of the term — ill-advised.

The events and conditions of the pre-war period are of considerable interest not only to historians, economists and military men, but also to the Soviet general public. It should be observed that it was a not infrequent practice at meetings and conferences [of various bodies] under Stalin to discuss questions and adopt decisions on them without making any written record, and sometimes even without any proper formalization of the decisions. It

H

also happened that after the discussion of particular questions the decision was adopted to 'entrust' such and such a person 'with introducing revised proposals taking account of the exchange of opinion which has occurred', but no record was kept as to who expressed what opinion. The result was that the one who presented the final version, who signed or sanctioned the 'revised' proposals or draft decisions, reflected as it were his own point of view . . .

It also happened, unfortunately, that a new leader began his activity not by studying existing experience, but with pronouncements and sermons and layings down of the 'line' brooking no question. A leader of this kind often worked by the rule that, since he was the boss, that meant he knew everything, and knew more than anyone else, including his predecessors. It was for this reason that he not infrequently dished up the same old thing as something new or, as they say, he discovered a long discovered 'America', sometimes renovating it slightly . . .

[Vannikov then turned to the question of Soviet weapons in World War II, stressing the vital role of the T-34 tank and its 75.2 mm. gun.]

Although many artillery weapons newly created for the Soviet Army were of high quality, they came very close to a sad fate in the immediate pre-war years. The new leadership of the Chief Artillery Directorate (GAU)[2] headed by G. I. Kulik and appointed in 1937 called in question the majority of newly created artillery weapons, and characterized the 152 mm. ML-20 howitzer (1937 version) as 'an act of sabotage',[3] meeting tactical requirements neither as gun nor howitzer (in a statement by Kulik, the Head of GAU, it was said to be 'neither a gun nor a howitzer'). Despite the fact that this howitzer had successfully passed the full test programme, had been adopted as a weapon, put into mass production and was evaluated as the most important in the whole weapons system, meeting all new tactical and technical requirements, the leaders of GAU demanded that it be put through a thorough retesting.

Retesting confirmed the good results, and furthermore towards the end of all this there began a certain sobering-up from the 'sabotageomania' and the ML-20 received just recognition again.

A few months before the Great Patriotic War the People's Commissariat for Armaments had to undergo some serious trials, which deserve closer examination. As I recall, at the beginning of

1941 the Head of GAU, G. I. Kulik, informed me that, according to intelligence reports, the German army was engaged in a rush reequipment of its armoured units with tanks possessing armour of increased thickness and improved quality, and that all our 45 to 76 mm. calibre artillery would be ineffective against them. Moreover they were supposed to have guns of over 100 mm. calibre. In connection with this the question was raised of terminating production of all variants of our 45 mm. to 76 mm. guns. It was proposed to employ the production facilities so released by producing 107 mm. guns, giving priority to a tank variant.

G. I. Kulik was a man given to rather wild enthusiasms, and an easy prey to rumours of all kinds, and for this reason we paid no special attention to the new project.

A few days later, however, G. I. Kulik, having armed himself with support from higher up, proposed that I should accompany him on a visit to Artillery Plant No. 92, in order to hold discussions on the spot with the designer V. G. Grabin and the leadership of the plant on the possibilities of rapidly designing a 107 mm. tank gun and organizing its production instead of the 76 mm. gun.

I refused to participate in the visit to the plant on the grounds that I had no directions from N. A. Voznesensky (the latter, as Chairman of the Economic Council of the Defence Industry, exercised supervision over the People's Commissariat for Armaments).[4] In answer to my question on the telephone N. A. Voznesensky said that he knew nothing about the matter, but I received permission to have G. I. Kulik provided with all the materials and explanations that might interest him at the plant.

The plant manager A. S. Elyan received an instruction from me to this effect, but at the same time it was stipulated that he was to enter into no obligations without the knowledge of the People's Commissariat of Armaments.

G. I. Kulik also decided on a visit to the Kirov plant in Leningrad accompanied by the designer and representatives of Artillery Plant No. 92, in order to continue his work with the participation of the Kirov tank-builders, and pressed for one of the leaders of the People's Commissariat for Armaments to take part in the visit.

We refused on this occasion as well, supposing that he would sort the matter out himself and in the long run put a stop to his ill-timed and dangerous project. But these hopes proved to be unjustified.

A few days after the events I have described J. V. Stalin summoned me. I found him alone. He had in his hands a note from G. I. Kulik. Showing it to me, he asked 'Have you read Comrade Kulik's note about the artillery? What have you to say about his proposal to arm the tanks with a 107 mm. gun?'

I had no knowledge of what was in the note, and Stalin informed me about it in a few words. Then he asked, 'What are your objections? Comrade Kulik says that you disagree with him'.

I explained the position of the People's Commissariat for Armaments as follows. Quite recently, in 1940, we knew that the majority of German tanks were armed with 37 or 55 mm. guns and a minority of them with 75 mm. guns. The calibre of tank and anti-tank guns corresponds as a rule with the armour of the tanks. It could therefore be considered that our 45 and 76 mm. tank and anti-tank artillery would be powerful enough. It was doubtful that in the brief period of one year the Germans could have made such a great leap in strengthening their tank equipment as was stated in the note. Moreover, should the need arise to increase the armour-piercing capacity of our medium calibre artillery, then the first thing to do was to raise the initial velocity of the 76 mm. guns. The transition to a higher calibre should not be begun with the 107 mm. gun. It would be more appropriate to take the bore [original says literally 'swinging part'] of the already available 85 mm. anti-aircraft gun, giving it greater initial velocity; it was already on strength and being turned out on large production lines. It was an unconvincing proposal to take out of production the 45 and 76 mm. guns in all their variants — battalion and divisional — since they served not only as anti-tank weapons, but were intended for combat against many other objectives (personnel, various obstructions, etc.) and were highly manoeuvrable. The 76 mm. ZIS gun, which had only recently been created and put into production, was the best contemporary gun.

Towards the end of my explanations A. A. Zhdanov entered.[5] Stalin turned to him and said: 'Vannikov here doesn't want to make 107 mm. guns for your Leningrad tanks. But these are very good guns, I know them from the Civil War'.

Zhdanov answered: 'Vannikov always opposes everything,

that's his work-style'. Then Stalin turned to Zhdanov: 'You're our chief artilleryman, we'll assign you a commission including Comrades Kulik, Vannikov, Goremykin [at that time People's Commissar for Munitions — B.L.V.] and whoever else you consider necessary to sort out this question'. And he again emphasized: 'But the 107 mm. gun is a good one'.

Stalin was talking about the field piece of the First World War period. This, apart from its calibre, had nothing in common with the gun needed for present-day tanks and for present-day battle conditions.[6] A comment casually dropped by Stalin usually settled the outcome of an issue. And that is how things turned out on this occasion as well.

In the course of preparing for the work of the commission there was a gathering in the People's Commissariat for Armaments of directors and designers of the artillery plants concerned. Once again we examined all the pros and cons in detail and from every possible angle and came to the conclusion that the proposal under consideration was not only inexpedient but for that period even dangerous.

The sitting of the commission under A. A. Zhdanov was attended by the following: from the military — G. I. Kulik, Major-General of Technical Troops M. M. Kaiukov and others; from the People's Commissariat for Armaments — Vannikov, Mirzakhanov (Deputy People's Commissar), Elyan (Director of Artillery Plant No. 92), Fradkin (Director of the Kalinin Plant) and others; and from the People's Commissariat for Munitions — Goremykin [the People's Commissar], his deputy, and others.

The chairman conducted the meeting incorrectly right from the start: he gave the military the opportunity of setting out their arguments in detail, while affording no such opportunity to the industry representatives. This way of conducting the conference compelled us to express our disapproval. At this A. A. Zhdanov harshly declared that Vannikov was engaging in sabotage, and ended with the phrase 'the dead man's dragging down the living'.

In reply I said to A. A. Zhdanov: 'You are disarming the army on the eve of a war'. He stood up, closed the meeting, and declared that he would complain about me to Stalin. After this everyone left, embarrassed by the way the work of the commission had ended.

I do not know what A. A. Zhdanov reported about all this,

only soon afterwards Stalin summoned me and showed me a Decision of the Central Committee and Council of People's Commissars in the spirit of Kulik's proposals which he had signed. I attempted to object, but Stalin stopped me and declared that he was already familiar with my objections and that we were guided by an unwillingness to switch over to the new product out of departmental interests at the expense of the general interests of the state. Tell the plant directors, he said, and in the first instance Elyan, that they are immediately to cease production of the 45 mm. and 76 mm. guns and to remove from their workshops all equipment not required for the production of the 107 mm. gun. This was to emphasize that there would be no reopening of the question.

So it was that shortly before the attack of fascist Germany on the Soviet Union it was decided to cease production of the 45 mm. and 76 mm. guns, the ones most needed for combat against the enemy's tanks. Without examining Kulik's completely groundless recommendations Stalin sanctioned this decision, which was to have severe consequences for the army.

We realized from the very first days of the war what an unforgivable mistake had been committed. The German-fascist armies advanced with the most heterogeneous and far from first class tank equipment, including captured French Renault tanks and obsolescent German T-I and T-II tanks, whose participation in the war had not been envisaged by the Germans. The information disposed of by Kulik, which guided Zhdanov and Stalin in adopting the mistaken decision to cease production of the 45 mm. and 76 mm. guns, had turned out to be baseless . . .

[Vannikov went on to discuss the underrating of mortars in the Soviet Union and the obstacles encountered by the brilliant Soviet mortar designer B. I. Shavyrin.]

Shortly before the war began Beria's henchmen cooked up a 'case' against our one and only senior designer of mortars B. I. Shavyrin. He was accused of sabotage and of malicious, intentional disorganization of the creation of mortars . . .

B. I. Shavyrin's arrest could have had dire consequences for our mortar weaponry. For this reason I came out determinedly in his defence. But at the beginning of June 1941 I was arrested myself.

The unjust arrest of a number of highly qualified specialists in industry and the central apparatus and their replacement by inadequately experienced cadres told heavily on the rearmament of the Soviet Army. The rapid turnover of cadres begot lack of accountability and of confidence and reduced responsibility, had a negative effect on production and technological discipline, and on the tempo of scientific and technical jobs, and consequently on the quality of production.

The dire lessons of the first months of the war taught us to value mortar weapons and their creators. Escaping arrest in connection with the outbreak of the war, B. I. Shavyrin continued working fruitfully on the new types of mortars so needed by our troops at the front. He is now a Hero of Socialist Labour.

A month had not passed after the outbreak of the war before the errors committed before the war in the field of armaments evoked pretty delicate consequences. Only thus can be explained the fact that I as former People's Commissar for Armaments was approached on behalf of Stalin, despite the fact that I was in solitary confinement on a strict prison regimen and accused of all the most grievous crimes, and asked to set out my ideas on how armaments should be developed and which weapons should be manufactured in which plants, taking account of the fact that the war had begun.

I worked for a few days in prison on this problem. I had no knowledge of the situation at the front. Isolated from everyone and everything, I was unable to imagine the position that had come about at the front and in the country. One could only suppose that there had been some small local reverses. I therefore reckoned that the questions posed for me had a long-range rather than an operative character. I also proceeded from the supposition that the decisions taken earlier (before my arrest), which I had disagreed with, had not turned out to be such grave errors. In the light of all this I compiled the required memorandum. This sorry event in my life ended with my release in July 1941. It bears witness to how unbearable for creative work was the set-up in the period of the cult of Stalin's personality.

NOTES

1. Extracts from 'Iz zapisok narkoma vooruzheniia: Vospominaniia trizhdy Geroia Sotsialisticheskogo Truda B. L. Vannikova' (From the 'Notes of a People's Commissar for Armaments: Memoirs of Thrice Hero of Socialist Labour B. L. Vannikov'), in *Kommunis-*

ticheskaia partiia v bor'be za uprochenie i razvitie sotsialisticheskogo obshchestva (1937 god - iun' 1941 goda) (*The Communist
Party in the Struggle to Consolidate and Develop Socialist Society
— 1937-June 1941*), Moscow, Gospolitizdat, 1962, pp. 370-6. These
memoirs were also printed in *Voenno-istoricheskii zhurnal* (Journal
of Military History) Moscow, No. 2, 1962, pp. 78-86. Vannikov
was People's Commissar for Armaments before World War II,
People's Commissar for Munitions during the war, and subsequently Minister ᶠor Agricultural Machine-building (the Commissariats were renamed Ministries in 1946). Editor's translation.

2. This came under the Defence Commissariat, headed at the time by
Voroshilov. Though Voroshilov was a member of the Politburo,
he does not appear to have become involved in the issue described
here by Vannikov.

3. 'Sabotage' (*vreditel'stvo*) was a standard ground for arrest during
the 1937-8 terror. GAU acquired a 'new leadership', headed by
Kulik, in 1937, and it may be assumed that their predecessors
were arrested.

4. Voznesensky was at that time Deputy Premier and Chairman of
the State Planning Commission; in February 1941 he became a
Candidate Member of the Politburo.

5. Zhdanov was a full member of the Politburo, holding concurrently
the posts of Secretary of the Central Committee and First Secretary
of the Leningrad Regional and City Committees. It is not clear
whether his involvement in this issue arose from his general role
as Stalin's righthand man on matters of internal policy (he
appears to have supplanted Kaganovich in this role in the late
1930s), or because the tanks were made in Leningrad.

6. Vannikov is suggesting here that Stalin was prone to make not only
arbitrary judgments, but unrealistic ones, based on inappropriate
or even absurd criteria. This is reminiscent of Khrushchev's
assertion that Stalin planned the military struggle against the Germans on a globe (*see* p. 58). Other witnesses, however, have
suggested a very different picture of Stalin's capacity for political
and tactical judgment during this period. Churchill, for instance,
was 'deeply impressed' by Stalin's 'swift and complete mastery of
a problem hitherto novel to him' (*see* Winston S. Churchill, *The
Second World War, Vol. IV: The Hinge of Fate*, London and
Boston, 1951, p. 434).

FURTHER READING

Of the several earlier editions of Khrushchev's 20th Congress report on Stalin, the following are particularly worthy of note: *The Anti-Stalin Campaign and International Communism,* edited by the Columbia University Russian Institute, New York, Columbia University Press, 1956 (includes statements and speeches by non-Soviet communists commenting on the issues raised by the report); Bertram D. Wolfe, *Khrushchev and Stalin's Ghost,* London, Atlantic Press, and New York, Praeger, 1957 (includes a long introduction, an extensive commentary, and a translation of the 16 documents on Stalin issued to the 20th Congress delegates); N. S. Khrushchev, *The Crimes of the Stalin Era: Special Report to the 20th Congress of the Communist Party of the Soviet Union,* New York, New Leader, 1956 (contains annotations by B. I. Nicolaevsky); and *The Dethronement of Stalin: Full Text of the Khrushchev Speech,* Manchester, *The Guardian,* 1956 (with a brief introduction and annotations by 'a student of Soviet affairs').

The best biography of Stalin is Isaac Deutscher, *Stalin: A Political Biography,* London, Oxford University Press, 1949; Revised Edition, Harmondsworth, Penguin, 1966. For the earlier period Leon Trotsky's *Stalin: An Appraisal of the Man and his Influence,* New York, Harper, 1941, and London, Hollis and Carter Ltd, 1947, is of particular importance. T. H. Rigby (ed.), *Stalin,* Englewood Cliffs, N.J., Prentice-Hall Inc., 1966, contains extracts from Stalin's writings and speeches, impressions written by foreign statesmen, diplomats and journalists, and analysis and evaluation by a number of scholars.

The most important non-Soviet account of Stalin as observed at close quarters in Milovan Djilas, *Conversations with Stalin,* New York, Harcourt, Brace and World, Inc., 1962, and Harmondsworth, Penguin, 1963. There are valuable sidelights on his character in his daughter's memoirs: Svetlana Alliluyeva, *Twenty Letters to a Friend,* London, Hutchinson, 1967.

Further Reading

Of the many excellent books on Soviet politics in the Stalin era and after, *see especially* Leonard Schapiro, *The Communist Party of the Soviet Union*, New York, Random House, and London, Eyre and Spottiswoode, 1960, London, Methuen, paperback, 1963; John A. Armstrong, *The Politics of Totalitarianism*, New York, Random House, 1961; R. Conquest, *Power and Policy in the U.S.S.R.*, London, Macmillan, and New York, St Martin's Press, 1961; Merle Fainsod, *Smolensk under Soviet Rule*, Cambridge, Mass., Harvard University Press, and London, Macmillan, 1958 and New York, Vintage paperback, 1963; Boris I. Nicolaevsky, *Power and the Soviet Elite*, (ed.) Janet D. Zagoria, New York, Praeger, 1965, and London, Pall Mall Press, 1966; Alec Nove, *Was Stalin Really Necessary? Some Problems of Soviet Political Economy*, London, Allen and Unwin, and New York, Praeger, 1964 (American edn entitled *Economic Rationality and Soviet Politics; or, Was Stalin Really Necessary?*); and Francis B. Randall, *Stalin's Russia: An Historical Reconsideration*, New York, Free Press, 1965.

For Stalin's own view of his era, *see History of the Communist Party of the Soviet Union (Bolsheviks): Short Course*, Moscow, Foreign Languages Publishing House, 1951.

On Khrushchev and the circumstances of the 20th Congress attack on Stalin, *see* Edward Crankshaw, *Khrushchev: A Career*, New York, The Viking Press, and London, Collins, 1966; Lazar Pistrak, *The Grand Tactician: Khrushchev's Rise to Power*, London, Thames and Hudson, and New York, Praeger, 1961; and George Paloczi-Horvath, *Khrushchev: the Road to Power*, London, Secker and Warburg, 1960; published in the U.S.A. under the title *Khrushchev: the Making of a Dictator*, Boston, Little Brown, 1960.

There is an extensive literature on the use of police terror under Stalin. Particularly recommended are Zbigniew K. Brzezinski, *The Permanent Purge*, Cambridge, Mass., Harvard University Press, 1956; F. Beck and W. Godin, *Russian Purge and The Extraction of Confession*, New York, The Viking Press, and London, Hurst & Blackett, 1951; and Alex Weissberg, *Conspiracy of Silence*, Hamish Hamilton, London, 1952; published in the U.S.A. under the title *Accused*, New York, Simon and Schuster, 1951.

INDEX

Abakumov, A. S., 63, 64, 88 n.27
Agriculture, 76-7
aktiv, 104, 107 n.7
Albania, 93-5
All-Russian Central Executive Committee, 41
Andreev, Andrei Andreevich, 69, 81
Anthem, Soviet national, 74
Anti-party group, 93, 96, 98-9, 102-4
Armaments, 54-5, 113-19

Bagramyan, (Marshal) Ivan K., 57
Balkars, 62
Baturina, N. K., 69
Benes, (President) Eduard, 99
Beria, Lavrentii Pavlovich (1899-1953), 12, 17, 45, 52, 63, 64, 67, 68-70, 85 n.6, 87 n.20 & 26, 88 n.28 & 30, 101
'Beria gang', 34, 50
Bliukher, Vasilii Konstantinovich (1889-1938), 99
Borba, 21
Borders, defence of, 53, 54, 55
Bozer, 53
Bukharin, Nikolai Ivanovich (1888-1938), 12, 45, 85 n.4, 109
'Bukharinites', 38, 71
Bulganin, Nikolai Aleksandrovich (1895-   ), 17, 80
Bureaucratization, 76

Capital punishment, abolition of, 41

Central Executive Committee, Presidium, refusal to consider petitions, 39
secretary of, 38
Chechens, 62
Cheka, 86 n.11
Chief Artillery Directorate (GAU), 114, 115
China, 19
and Albania, 93
and U.S.S.R., 93
Chou En-lai, 94
Chubar, V. Ya. (1891-1941), 48, 51, 66, 87 n.18, 101
Chudov, 47
Churchill, Sir Winston Spencer, and view of Stalin, 120 n.6
and warning to Stalin, 53
Civil War, 75
Collegiality, 34-5
Collective farms *see* kolkhoz
Collective leadership *see* Collegiality *and* Communist party, collective leadership
Commissars, Commissariats *see* Council of People's Commissars
Commission on artillery weapons, 117
Communist party
Central Committee, 17, 24-5, 34, 44, 51, 68, 69, 70, 82, 84, 102-5, 110-18
and accusations against Beria, 68
expulsion of members of, 43

First Secretary, 15, 17, 93, 99

General Secretary, 26, 110

investigations by, 63

Khrushchev's supporters on, 14

Organizational Bureau, 31, 68

overruling of Presidium by, 93

plenary sessions of, 11, 36, 40, 42, 49, 67, 80, 81, 85 n.7

Political Bureau, 11, 17, 31, 38, 40, 49, 63, 64, 67, 79-82, 89 n.39

Presidium, 37, 74, 82, 89 n.39, 93

investigation of purges by, 13, 37, 100

Secretary, 63

Collective leadership in, 15, 78, 102-4, 108 n.9

Congress, 35-36

7th (1918), 35

8th (1919), 35

9th (1920), 35

10th (1921), 35, 42

17th (1934), 29, 36, 37-8, 42

18th (1939), 36

19th (1952), 36

20th (1956), 11, 13, 94, 96, 98, 99, 102, 104

editions of Khrushchev's 'secret speech', 20-1

impact of, 18-19

21st (1959), 93

22nd (1961), 93, 94, 108 n.9

handling differences within, 95-6

history of, 73, 84, 89 n.41, 98

Party, Central Committee (Central Control Commission, Committee of

Party and State Control), 31

expulsion of members of, 43

Party Programme, 102, 103

Party Rules, 42-3, 102, 103, 108 n.9

Revision Commission, 105

Conferences, procedure at, 113-14

Confessions, 39, 43-8 (*see also* Purges *and* Torture)

Constitution, U.S.S.R., 84

Control Commission *see* Communist party, Central Committee, Party Control Committee

Conversations with Stalin, 113

Council of Ministers (1946-   )

Committee of State Security (KGB), 68, 86 n.11

First Deputy Chairman of, 62, 67

Minister of State Security (MGB), 66

State Planning Commission (Gosplan), Chairman of, 81, 120 n.4

Council of People's Commissars (1917-46), 44, 113-19

Economic Council of the Defence Industry, Chairman of, 115

People's Commissariat for Armaments, 113-19

People's Commissariat for Health, 67

People's Commissariat for Internal Affairs (NKVD), 40, 46, 86 n.11, 101

archives of, 37

attacks on, 50

falsification of cases by, 47-9

heads of, 51

Stalin on, 40, 50-1

People's Commissariat for Munitions, 117
Cripps, Sir Stafford, 54
Cult of the individual, theoretical explanations of, 15-17, 108 n.9
Decision-making under Stalin, 22 n.1, 80, 113-19 (*see also* Communist party)
Deficiencies of Party work and methods for the liquidation of the Trotskyites and other double-dealers, 41
Denikin, Anton Ivanovich (1872-1947), 41
Deportations, 62, 87 n.25
De-Stalinization, 93
Djilas, Milovan, 113
'doctor-plotters affair', 66-7, 88 n.30
Dzerzhinsky, Felix Edmundovich (1877-1926), 41

Egorov, 99
Eideman, 99
Eikhe, R. I. (1890-1940), 79, 86 n.14, 101
    investigation of case of, 43-6
Elyan, A. S., 115, 117, 118
Emelyanov, V. S., 22 n.1
Engels, Friedrich (1820-95), 24, 72, 105

'The Fall of Berlin' (film), 60
Films, 60, 75
Foreign relations
    Albania, 93
    China, 19, 93
    Stalin's role in, 65-6
    U.S.S.R. and Yugoslavia, 65-6
Fradkin, 117

GAU *see* Chief Artillery Directorate
Georgia, 64-5, 88 n.28
Golubiev, 69

Gorbatov, 57
Goremykin, P. N., 117
GPU, 86 n.11

Hitler, Adolf, 53

Ignatiev, Semen Denisovich, 66, 88 n.30
Ingushi, deportation of, 62

Kabakov, 48
Kabardino-Balkar Autonomous Republic, 62
Kaganovich, Lazar' Moiseevich (1893-   ), 14, 17, 22 n.2, 39, 68, 89 n.40, 95, 100, 102, 103, 104, 107 n.5, 120 n.5
Kaiukov, M. M., 117
Kalmyk Autonomous Republic, 62
Kamenev, Lev Borisovich (1883-1936), 27, 32, 33, 96, 109
'Kamenevites', 71
Kaminsky, 67, 68
Karachai, deportation of, 62
Karpov, 42
Kartvelishvili-Lavrentiev, Lavrentii Iosifovich (1891-1938), 68, 69
Kedrov, M. S. (1878-1941), 69, 88 n.33
Kerensky, Aleksandr Fedorovich (1881-   ), 32
KGB *see* Council of Ministers, Committee of State Security
Khlopov, 53
Khrushchev, Nikita Sergeevich (1894-   ), 22 n.2, 80, 85 n.6, 87 n.26, 88 n.28, 89 n.37, 107 n.8, 110
    and purges, 85 n.8
    challenge to, 93
    fall of, 94
    rise to power of, 14
Kiev radio, 83

Kirov, Sergei Mironovich (1886-1934), 110, 112 n.4
  assassination of, 38, 39, 97-8, 111
Kirponos, 55
Kolkhoz, 76-7
Komarov, 47
Kork, 99
Kosarev, A. V. (1903-39), 48, 50, 87 n.19
Kosior, S. V. (1889-1939), 48, 49, 50, 65, 79, 83, 86 n.17, 101
Kozlov, Frol Romanovich (1908-), 94
Krupskaya, Nadezhda Konstantinovna (1869-1939) and Stalin, 27-8
Kulik, G. I., 114-18
Kuznetsov, A. A. (1905-49), 62, 64, 66, 80, 88 n.26, 101

Leadership, communist view of, 104-6, 107 n.9
  defects under Stalin of, 78, 114
Lenin, Vladimir Il'yich (1870-1924), 71, 72, 74, 75, 78, 79, 82, 96, 101, 105, 106, 110
  and Central Committee, 35
  and opposition, 33
  and Political Bureau, 35
  letter to Stalin, 27-8
  on capital punishment, 41
  on Central Committee, 24-5
  on collegiality, 34-5
  on cult of the individual, 24
  on duties of Control Commission, 31
  on party and leadership, 24-5
  on Secretary-General, 26
  on Stalin, 26
  on violence, 41
  treatment of Zinoviev and Kamenev, 32-3
Lenin Prizes for educational work, 75

Leningrad, 53, 55, 120 n.5
'Leningrad affair', 62-4, 87 n.26

Malenkov, Georgii Maksimilianovich (1902-), 12, 14, 17, 22 n.2, 55, 58, 88 n.26, 95, 102, 104, 107 n.5
Marx, Karl (1818-93), 24, 72, 105
Meetings *see* Conferences
Meretskov, Kirill Afanas'evich (1897-), 57
Mezhlauk, Valerii Ivanovich (1893-1938), 45
MGB, 86 n.11
Mikoyan, Anastas Ivanovich (1895-), 14, 17, 59, 68, 81
Military *see* Purges *and* World War II
Military Collegium of Supreme Court, 46, 48, 49, 70
Military equipment *see* Armaments
'Mingrelian affair', 64-5, 88 n.30
Minority groups *see* National minorities
Mirzakhanov, 117
Molotov, Viacheslav Mikhailovich (1890-), 14, 22 n.2, 39, 81, 89 n.40, 95, 97, 100, 102, 104, 107 n.5
Monuments to Stalin, 74
Moscow, 52, 53
MTS (Machine and Tractor Stations), 77
Mussavat, 67, 88 n.31
MVD, 86 n.11

Naming of places after leaders, 82-3, 89 n.40
National minorities, deportation of, 62,
Nationalism in Georgia, 64, 65
New Economic Policy, 35
Nikolaev (Kirov's assassin), 39

Nikolaevsky, Boris, 109
NKGB, 86 n.11
NKVD *see* Council of People's Commissars, Commissariat for Internal Affairs
Novaia Zhizn', 32

October Revolution
  disclosure of plans for, 32
  Stalin's role in, 75
OGPU, 40, 86 n.11
'On Party Unity', 35
Opposition groups, 29, 30, 38, 48, 71, 79, 109
  danger to party from, 40
  voting for, 40 (*see also* Bukharinites; Kamenevites: Trotskyites; Zinovievites)
Opposition to Khrushchev, 93-4
Ordzhonikidze, Grigorii Konstantinovich (1886-1937), 69, 70, 88 n.32, 101

Palace of Soviets, 74, 89 n.36
People's Commissars and Commissariats *see* Council of People's Commissars
Podlas, 57
Politburo *see* Communist party, Central Committee, Political Bureau
Ponomarev, B. N. (1905-), 89 n.41
Popkov, P. S. (1903-49), 62, 88 n.26
Poskrebyshev, A. N., 60, 87 n.24
Postyshev, P. P. (1888-1940), 42, 48, 50, 65, 79, 80, 86 n.13, 101
Power and the Soviet Elite, 109
Pozern, 47
Purges, 11, 29, 30, 40, 49, 69-70, 97, 100, 120 n.3
  and first secretaries of party committees, 48

decrease in arrests (1939), 50
  directives on, 39
  effects of, 49, 56, 76, 99, 119
  'enemy of the people', 30
  expulsion of CC members, 43
  fabrication of cases in, 43-52
  increase in arrests (1936-7), 42
  in Georgia, 64-5, 88 n.28
  in Ukraine, 17
  investigation of, 37, 38
  involvement of Presidium members in, 98
  'Leningrad affair', 62-4
  Leningrad Centre, 47-8
  of armed forces, 56-7, 87 n.21
  of delegates and CC members elected at 17th Congress, 37-8, 111
  of 'doctor-plotters', 66-7
  of Political Bureau members, 80, 81-2
  of specialists, 119
  pretexts for, 111
  questioning of, 42
  rehabilitation of victims of, 49, 100-2
  theoretical justification of, 41
  (*see also* Torture; Confessions)

Rodionov, M. I., 62, 80, 88 n.26
Rodos, 51-2
Rodzyanko, 32
Rokossovsky, Konstantin Konstantinovich (1896-), 56-7
Rozenblum, 47-8
Rudzutak, Ya. E. (1887-1938), 46, 47, 50, 79, 86 n.15, 101
Rukhimovich, 45
Rykov, Aleksei Ivanovich (1881-1938), 109

Shaposhnikova, 47
Shaumyan, L., 12, 109

Shavyrin, B. I., 118, 119
Shelepin, Aleksandr Nikolaevich (1918-   ), 98, 100, 107 n.5
Short Biography (Stalin), 71, 73, 75
The Short Course of the History of the All-Union Communist Party (Bolsheviks), 73
Smorodin, 47
Snegov, declaration to Central Committee by, 68
Sovkhoz, 76-7
Stalin
    ability, 120 n.6
    character of, 26-9
    handling of opposition by, 34
    responsibility for purges, 49
    role in World War II, 52-61
    self-glorification, 71-5, 77
Stalin Prizes, 74
Stalingrad, 52
Svanidze, Alyosha, 101

Taxes, 77
Timashuk, 66
Tito, Josif Broz (1892-   ), 13, 65, 66
Togliatti, Palmiro, 19
Tomsky, Mikhail Pavlovich (1880-1936), 109
Torture, 50, 52, 66-7, 70, 100
'Trotskyites', 33, 38, 40, 42, 44, 48, 71, 79
Tukhachevsky, Mikhail Nikolaevich (1893-1937), 99-100
Turkey, 64, 65

Uborevich, 99, 100
Ugarov, 47
'The Unforgettable Year of 1919' (film), 75
'Ural uprising', 48
Ushakov, 45

Vannikov, B. L. (1897-1962), 113, 120 n.1
Vasilevsky, Aleksandr Mikhailovich (1895-   ), 58
Vinogradov, 66
Vorontsov, 53
Voroshilov, Kliment Efremovich (1881-   ), 22 n.2, 75, 81, 89 n.40, 96, 97, 100, 107 n.5, 120 n.2
Voznesensky, Nikolai Alekseevich (1903-50), 62, 64, 66, 80, 81, 88 n.26, 101, 115, 120 n.4

World War II, 60, 61
    and plenums of Central Committee, 36
    and soviet weapons, 114-19
    German preparations and attack, 52-6
    Stalin's role in, 52-61

Yagoda, Genrikh Grigorievich (1891-1938), 40
Yakir, Iona Emmanuilovich (1861-1937), 99-100
Yenukidze, Avel' Safronovich (1877-?), 38, 110
Yezhov, Nikolai Ivanovich (1895-1939?), 40, 42, 49, 87 n.20
Yugoslavia, 65-6

Zakovsky, 47, 48
Zhdanov, Andrei Aleksandrovich (1896-1948), 39, 87 n.26, 116, 117, 118, 120 n.5
Zhukov, (Marshal) Georgii Konstantinovich, 59-60, 87 n.22
Zinoviev, Georgii Evseevich (1883-1936), 27, 32, 33, 96, 109
'Zinovievites', 38, 40, 71, 79